BORDERLANDS

South Yorkshire in the Anglo-Saxon and Viking Periods, AD 450–1066

This book is dedicated to those who like to remove borders rather than create them.

BORDERLANDS

SOUTH YORKSHIRE IN
THE ANGLO-SAXON AND VIKING
PERIODS, AD 450–1066

PHIL SIDEBOTTOM

PEN & SWORD
HISTORY

AN IMPRINT OF PEN & SWORD BOOKS LTD.
YORKSHIRE – PHILADELPHIA

First published in Great Britain in 2023 by
PEN AND SWORD HISTORY
An imprint of
Pen & Sword Books Ltd
Yorkshire – Philadelphia

ISBN 978 1 39906 556 6

Typeset in Times New Roman 12/16 by
SJmagic DESIGN SERVICES, India.
Printed and bound in the UK by CPI Group (UK) Ltd.

Pen & Sword Books Limited incorporates the imprints of Atlas, Archaeology,
Aviation, Discovery, Family History, Fiction, History, Maritime, Military,
Military Classics, Politics, Select, Transport, True Crime, Air World, Frontline
Publishing, Leo Cooper, Remember When, Seaforth Publishing, The Praetorian
Press, Wharncliffe Local History, Wharncliffe Transport, Wharncliffe True Crime
and White Owl.

For a complete list of Pen & Sword titles please contact
PEN & SWORD BOOKS LIMITED
George House, Units 12 & 13, Beevor Street, Off Pontefract Road,
Barnsley, South Yorkshire, S71 1HN, England
E-mail: enquiries@pen-and-sword.co.uk
Website: www.pen-and-sword.co.uk

Or
PEN AND SWORD BOOKS
1950 Lawrence Rd, Havertown, PA 19083, USA
E-mail: Uspen-and-sword@casematepublishers.com
Website: www.penandswordbooks.com

Contents

Introduction

South Yorkshire has a unique place in the story of the struggles between the emerging kingdoms of Northumbria and Mercia, the area witnessing several battles in this process. Although the terms 'Anglo-Saxon' and 'Viking' will have been used in this book, the evidence for Germanic and Scandinavian incomers remained limited in South Yorkshire for some time and the native or 'British' character of much of the county seems to linger on through the ages. The purpose of this investigation is to synthesize the available information of the period from the end of Roman occupation of South Yorkshire to the Norman Conquest. Historically, there is not a lot of such information, so we have to rely on a whole host of alternative evidence, from archaeological investigation through to place-name and even dialect analysis in this period, which is aptly known as the 'Dark Ages'. The period spans almost 700 years, during which time the region was transformed from what one might call the post-Roman Iron Age, with its dispersed settlements, into something more familiar to us, a medieval landscape with villages, churches and open strip fields.

South Yorkshire is, of course, not an old county. It came into being as recently as 1974, but then was abolished as a unitary authority in 1986, with administration devolving to the four metropolitan boroughs of Barnsley, Doncaster, Rotherham and Sheffield. That said, perhaps there was always a 'south Yorkshire', in the sense that the region always found itself an area forming the borderland between various rival factions through time, which gave it a unique character. You could say that today, South Yorkshire is where the North meets the Midlands, and that in itself is a reflection of its borderland status following its turbulent past. South Yorkshire was part of the old West Riding of Yorkshire, a '*thriding*' (meaning 'a third part') created, as far as we know, by the Scandinavian administration based in York. But even the *thriding* was probably a relatively late creation of the nominal Anglo-Saxon period, and it is only known to us – as are many other aspects of the Anglo-Saxon period – from the *Domesday* survey

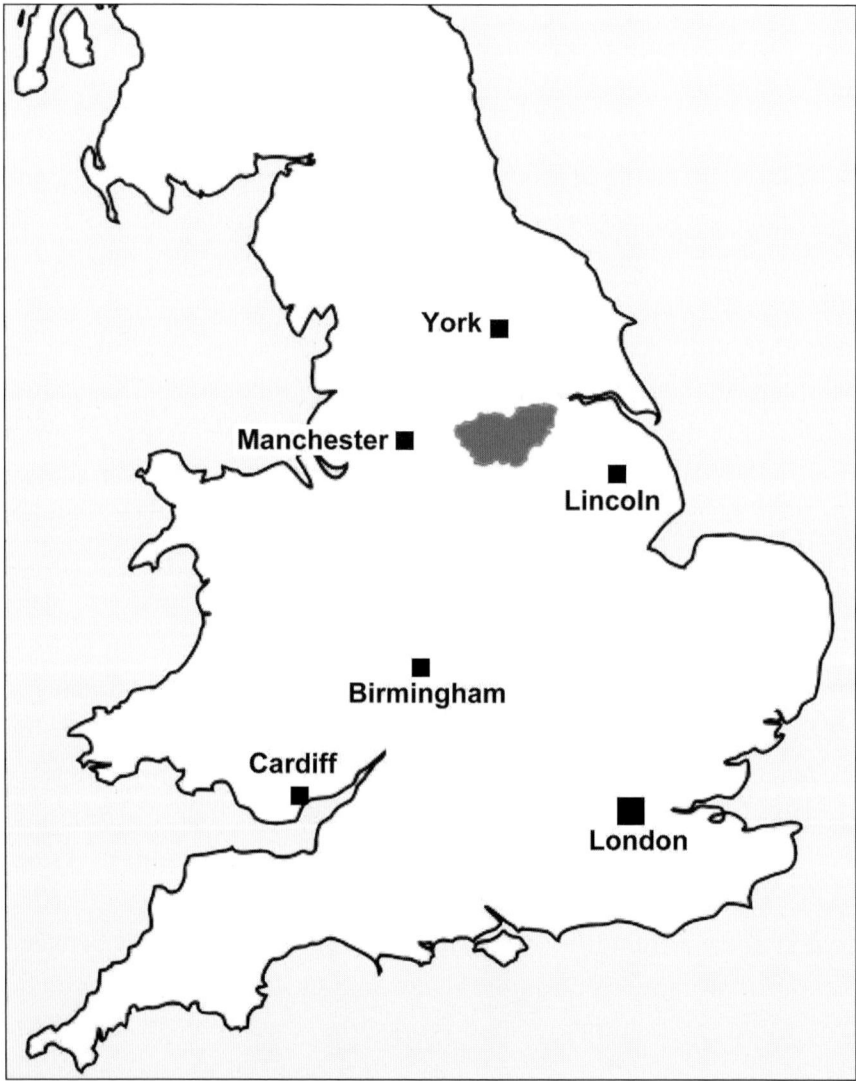

Fig. 1: The location of South Yorkshire.

of 1086. Before that time, the South Yorkshire region is shrouded in mystery, yet although there is little documentary evidence available to help us understand the county between the fifth and eleventh centuries, this book is an attempt to shed a little light on this otherwise 'dark' period of history.

Chapter 1

The Topography, Geology and Economy of South Yorkshire

The geology of South Yorkshire varies from the older, Carboniferous rocks of the southern Pennines in the west of the county, to the relatively younger Triassic bedrock in the east, much of which is overlain by peaty deposits and river alluvium. The contrast is quite dramatic: in the west, the land rises to in excess of 500 metres on the high rugged landscape above Sheffield, but to the east of Doncaster, the land is quite flat and lies close to sea level.

The Millstone Grit uplands in the west have poorly drained and largely depleted soils only suitable for limited livestock farming. Settlements are relatively small in an area characterized by hill farms on the eastern slopes of the Pennines, with heather moorland on the higher ground. Further east, the clay soils of the Coal Measures (lower, middle and upper) in some areas are prone to waterlogging, but arable cultivation and pasture have been prevalent in this area. However, the Coal Measures landscape has been dominated in the last century or two by industrialization and mineral extraction. In contrast, the ridge of Magnesian Limestone to the east of the Coal Measures is relatively well-drained and provides good arable land, although it occupies a north–south strip only 4–5km wide.

In the east of the county, the bedrock is of Sherwood Sandstone, normally forming lighter, sandy soils, but much of the land between Doncaster and east of Tickhill is peaty and now artificially drained. Up to the seventeenth century, when reclamation measures were taken in earnest – largely by the Dutch engineer Cornelius Vermuyden – this area was part of the wetlands of the Humberhead Levels, an area of fens, lakes and shallow river channels stretching from the Humber estuary to the lowlands east of Maltby (Van de Noort, 2003). The Levels, together with the fen and carr (vegetation on marshy ground) along the courses of the rivers Idle and Ryton, have, in the past, formed a topographical barrier in the east of the county; during the post-Roman period, it is generally accepted that a cooler and wetter climate prevailed (Stein, 2019, p.3), which no doubt contributed to this environmental barrier. The area of fens in the east of present-day South Yorkshire, north Nottinghamshire and north Lincolnshire was the third largest in England before drainage gradually reduced it to almost nothing by the early-twentieth century. The legacy of the fen – the Humberhead Levels – is shown in Fig. 3, where large areas of peat and alluvium are the residual of the wetlands forming the eastern border to the county, reconstructed by Rotherham and Harrison (2006). The archaeological evidence from the Humberhead Levels project (Van de Noort, 2003) suggests that there was little or no settlement on the fens during the post-Roman period, in contrast to that in the previous Roman period. It is concluded that the area was, in the post-Roman period, probably used primarily to graze livestock destined for markets at Doncaster, York or Lincoln (*ibid.*, pp.259–60).

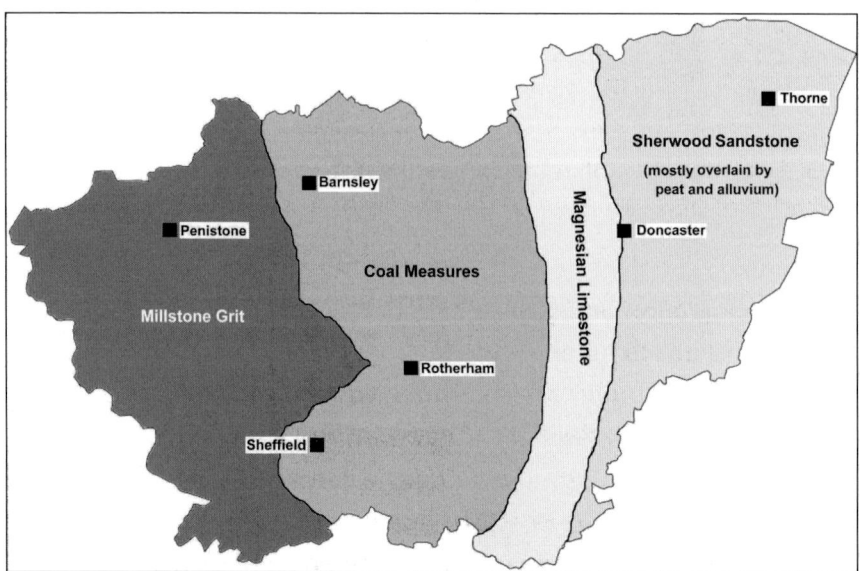

Fig. 2: The simplified geology of South Yorkshire.

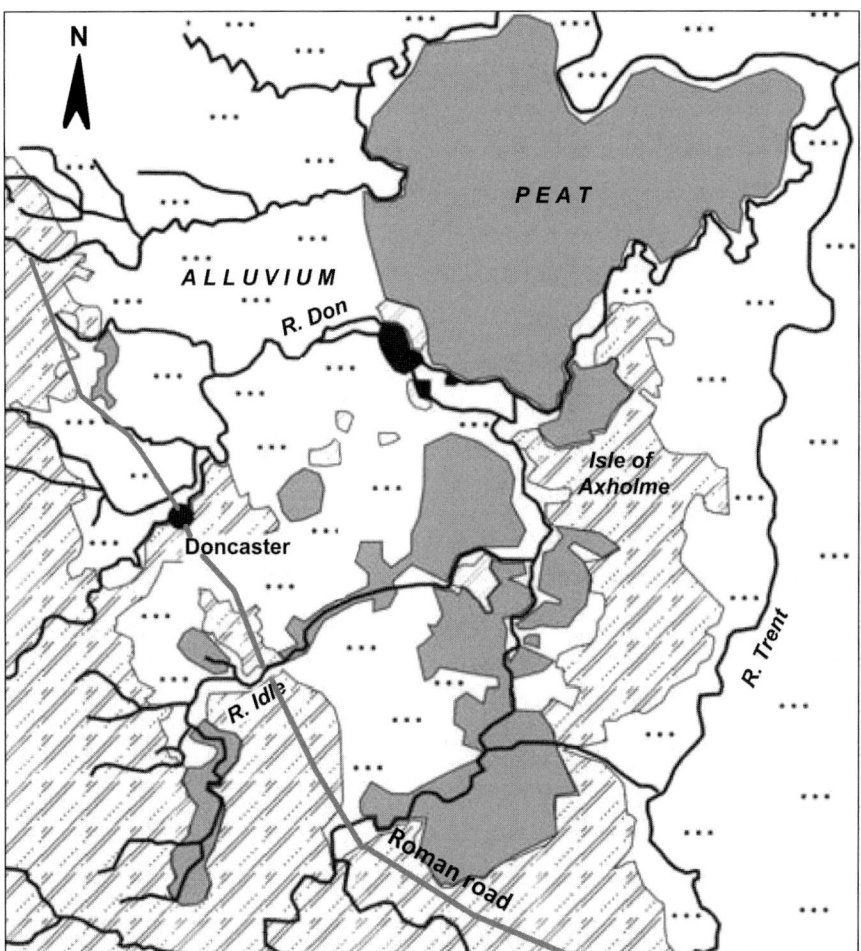

Fig. 3: Areas of peat and alluvium forming the residual of the Humberhead Levels (based on Rotherham and Harrison, 2006).

The topography and geology of the South Yorkshire landscape is typical of much of the old West Riding which extends north-westwards from South Yorkshire and no doubt once fostered a shared value of land management and economic production across the entire region. Sheep farming on the western uplands and cattle rearing on the Coal Measures quite possibly formed the backbone of the South Yorkshire post-Roman economy, with limited arable capability on the Magnesian Limestone ridge and in some more suitable areas of the

Coal Measures. However, elsewhere, the Triassic Sandstone regions of the north Midlands to the south and the rich arable lands of the Vale of York to the north-east were more suited to arable production and no doubt formed the focus of economic production in these regions. Both of these 'arable-focussed' areas became central to the emerging kingdoms of Deira in the north (the southern component of the kingdom of Northumbria) and Mercia to the south.

The writer has argued elsewhere (see, for example, Sidebottom, 2020) that economic 'ecozones' were very important in determining the parameters of the early, smaller land units, quite a few of which were included in the *Tribal Hidage*, a document probably dating from the Middle Saxon period which listed all the smaller, and perhaps once independent, land units which eventually comprised the kingdom of Mercia and its neighbours; the *Tribal Hidage* will be returned to later. The South Yorkshire post-Roman landscape was, then, perhaps one predominantly of livestock husbandry rather than arable production, which was likely to have been the case since the Iron Age if not before. This diversity of economic activity between regions seemingly had a major role to play in the settlement preferences of the Germanic incomers – the Saxons – and later the Scandinavians.

That is not to say that livestock exclusively formed the economy in western Yorkshire; there were other commodities which were likely to have been in relative abundance in the southern Yorkshire region. Bede mentions 'Elmet Wood' which was seemingly close to *Campodonum*, which may have been Doncaster (Higham, 1993a, p.86) or possibly Slack, near Hebden Bridge, in West Yorkshire (Sherley-Price, 1955, p.132). Woodland, and therefore timber, is another commodity which was probably in demand in the arable lands elsewhere. At Wharncliffe, near Sheffield, a quernstone 'factory' is known where extensive late Iron Age and Romano-British rotary grinding querns were manufactured, seemingly in vast quantities. The distribution of these artefacts still covers 72 hectares, despite it comprising only the residual broken stones in various stages of completion (Historic England, 2020). Millstone Grit, which was the stone type used for their manufacture, was extensively available in the west of the county. From personal experience, hone-stones made from Pennine sandstone are frequently found in Lincolnshire and no doubt elsewhere; sharpening stones would have been a commodity which was seemingly traded widely through the Anglo-Saxon period and beyond. Whetstones have been recovered from graves from the fifth to the eighth centuries, and appear to have been particularly popular in the seventh century. An example was found in a burial context at Adwick-le-Street in 2007 (McKinley, 2016, p.105), as discussed later.

The lowlands in the east of the county, whilst of little use for most agriculture, would have provided a rich source of wildfowl, fish and other aquatic commodities. The wetlands' economic importance is well attested to, especially in the years before Vermuyden's drainage schemes (Rotherham and Harrison, 2006, p.13). Sheffield developed its early metal economy on the available ironstone, wood for smelting and the high ground and 'edges' of the west, suitable areas for providing the draft for furnaces and water power. Pottery was produced extensively in the Roman period in South Yorkshire, although Dark Age ceramic artefacts are rare so this resource apparently did not feature strongly in the local economy and appears to have been severely limited before the Norman Conquest. Indeed, research into local pottery by Chris Cumberpatch has suggested that the nominal Anglo-Saxon period in South Yorkshire was largely aceramic (Cumberpatch, 2011), no doubt linked to the economic mode of production and consumption of the period. These are a few – perhaps just the obvious ones – of the economic resources available to the people of post-Roman South Yorkshire, and they were, by and large, absent or in limited supply in the arable lands of the Vale of York or in the north Midlands. Therefore, there was a quite obvious potential for a symbiotic relationship developing between the southern Pennine region and other groups of people occupying different ecozones.

Although now a little dated, the study by Faull and Moorhouse (1981) of the archaeological resource in West Yorkshire is still an invaluable synthesis and much of their work is pertinent today. They make the point that the post-Roman environment is largely surmised through place-name evidence but that this has a number of limitations, especially that place-names recorded by 1086 – when we first know of most of them – were not by then necessarily nucleated settlements, as they became later, and so may have occupied a different geography during the post-Roman and later Saxon periods. The lack of a recognizable pottery sequence for the post-Roman period means that field-walking exercises are frustrated by inconclusive results, and it is almost certain that Dark Age sites have not been identified due to lack of indicative material culture. That said, there are generalities that no doubt determined settlement locations and the nature of localized economies. The basic considerations which apply to any period are soils, drainage, climate, access to land suitable for ploughing, access to water, fuel and building materials (Faull and Moorhouse, 1981, pp.60–61). All of these determined settlement patterns, but these commodities also forged local identity and provided the means to trade with other groups with different resources, perhaps not always on an equal basis.

Mason and Williamson (2017) also considered that social identity in the post-Roman period was shaped by landscape geography, and this same argument has been advanced by the writer with regard to the *Pecsaetna*, the Anglo-Saxon limestone Peak District land unit. Mason and Williamson's studies investigated the East Anglian chalklands, which led them to suggest that communities were focused on particular valleys, or valley systems, developing identities distinct from those dwelling on the other side of a watershed (2017, p.85). Such an idea of topographical-determinism may have some merit for the area considered here. Given that South Yorkshire, West Yorkshire and the Pennine range in general largely comprise a similar ecozone, some physical separation might have been provided by the larger Yorkshire rivers which tend to travel from west to east (principally the Aire, Wharfe, Calder and Don). The south-eastern Pennine landscape was geographically bounded by the hostile and rugged terrain of the

Millstone Grit uplands in the west and curtailed by the wetlands east of Doncaster. The main question is whether this part of western Yorkshire can be compared with the East Anglian chalklands. Was the region really a collection of small tribal units in the early Saxon period, as Mason and Williamson's study would imply, or was there far more homogeny between peoples of southern Yorkshire? This idea will be explored later.

The Roman background to the South Yorkshire region

The Dark Ages are generally said to begin in AD 410, when the Roman military withdrew support from Britain. However, in reality it began well before the early fifth century. The extent of Romanization in Britain was variable. The south and east of England were well immersed in Roman culture – villas, towns and settlements, often owned and run by the retired military. But in the north, and especially in Pennine Yorkshire, Romanization was far less established. By the third century AD, South Yorkshire appears to have been in the region known to the Romans as *Britannia Secunda* (Higham, 1993a, p.50), an area where militarization took precedence over urbanization. This apparent lesser state of Roman society is almost certainly why contemporary documentation is lacking for the region.

Although we know little about Roman-period tribal boundaries, contemporary sources suggest that much of the region may have been included in the territorial jurisdiction of the Brigantes, a tribal unit which offered particular resistance to Roman advances in Britain and accentuated military tensions in northern England. Chadwick notes that after *c.* AD 120, South Yorkshire may have become incorporated within the administration of a *civitas* based at Aldborough (Isurium Brigantium), now in North Yorkshire. However, it is possible that the area of the county south-east of the River Don might have been part of the *civitas* of the Corieltauvi/Coritani, which was centred at

Leicester (*Ratae Corieltauvorum*) (Chadwick, 2019, p.6; Ottaway, 2019). Present-day Lincolnshire was also Corieltauvian territory, and their coinage has been found in South Yorkshire too (Buckland, 1986, pp.5–6). Although there is no detailed historical reference and the archaeological evidence has little to add, there is some merit in seeing at least part of South Yorkshire being Corieltauvian territory, especially in terms of territorial control after the collapse of Roman society; this aspect will be returned to later. However, these relatively large territorial units, such as the Brigantes or the Corielauvi, were Roman administrative areas and may have included smaller Iron Age people-groups of which we know nothing. To what extent these tribal units influenced post-Roman divisions – for example, those expressed in the document known as the *Tribal Hidage* (see below) – is unknown, but it is likely that when the Roman administration collapsed, some reversion to former tribalism was inevitable. Elmet, that area of former Brigantian territory now in West and South Yorkshire, is known to us from the Anglo-Saxon period from the writings of Bede (Sherley-Price, 1955) and other documentary sources. It was probably one of a series of British tribal units that extended northwards from the southern Pennines, and possibly predated the Roman period as a unit of the Brigantes, formed from a confederation of tribes rather than a single polity (Gruffydd, 1994, pp.63–64).

Our knowledge of the principal Roman centres in the region is variable. As part of the Roman occupation in adjacent areas such as present-day Nottinghamshire, Lincolnshire and East Yorkshire, a network of forts and stations were developed, all linked by roads with small settlements, rural villas and an increasingly-Romanized material culture. Again, we see a division between good arable lands and those that were not so good, and consequently the effect of Roman occupation was different in Pennine Yorkshire. Few villas have been identified here, and the area west and north-west of the River Don seems to have been far less Romanized in terms of settlement and material culture use than that south of the Don. However, as discussed above, the latter was probably not Brigantian, and was therefore more amenable to Romanization. In South Yorkshire, there was a fortress at Rossington and forts with attendant *vici* at Templeborough and Doncaster (*Danum*), with perhaps a *vicus* or roadside settlement at Thorpe Audlin, along with pottery production at Rossington Bridge which became a significant regional industry during the Roman period (Chadwick, 2019, p.11). A small fort may have existed at Long Sandall, some 5km north-east of Doncaster, predating that at *Danum* (Ottaway, 2019).

Further afield, there was a major Roman settlement at Castleford to the north (Chadwick, 2019, p.11), and to the south, now in northern Derbyshire, was the fort at Brough-on-Noe (*Navio*) near Hope (a rare 'green-field' monument) and that at Chesterfield (Dearne, 1990, p,99; Taylor, 2006, p.144). Most of the forts had a *vicus* attached to them, some developing into civilian centres which outlived the garrisons of the forts (Dearne, 1990, pp.96–113). Some of the main Roman centres may have endured into the post-Roman period, standing as they did on the convergence of roads and located in strategic locations, making them obvious administrative centres. In this region, Brough-on-Noe, Doncaster and Castleford may have remained as focal centres, in some form or another, after the collapse of the Roman economy.

Many Roman communication routes, especially the principal road system, continued through the Anglo-Saxon period, where the term 'street' was frequently used to denote a Roman highway. Roman roads became increasingly useful to the emerging kingdoms of Anglo-Saxon England, with relatively large armies able to move swiftly across the landscape on well-known and direct routes. Their focal points, periodic fortifications and strategic geography served both Roman and Saxon armies alike. In Britain, Roman military roads have been researched over a long period of time (see Margary, 1973) and a reasonable assessment of their courses has been established, but no doubt lesser trackways and pre-existing routes played an equally important role (Dearne, 1990, p.60), and many of these are likely to have survived to the present.

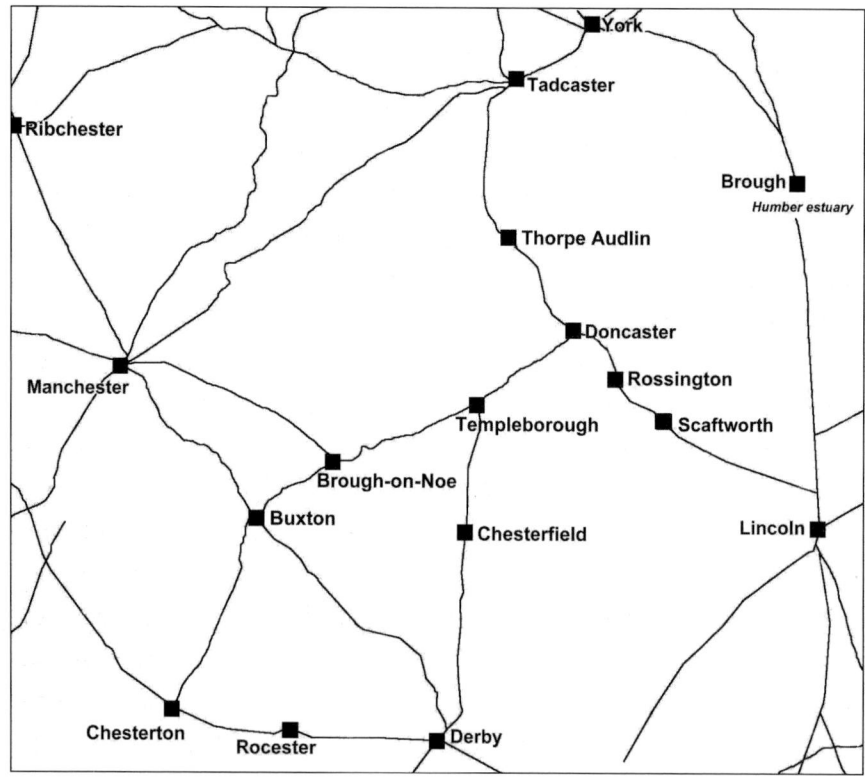

Fig. 4: Roman roads in the region.

Consequently, the most significant routes in the region were the well-maintained military roads linking the forts and fortlets. Of particular note are the Roman roads in northern Derbyshire, Cheshire and South Yorkshire, roads linking the forts at Manchester (*Mancunium*) in the west, through Glossop (*Melandra*), Brough-on-Noe (*Navio*) in the northern Peak District, Templeborough near Rotherham and on to Doncaster in the east. All of these military installations, and the roads linking them, generally formed a largely east–west orientation, which was in part intended to seal off the southern Pennines, and thereby the Brigantes to the north if need be. This meant that only two major routes travelled northwards into what became the Anglo-Saxon kingdom of Northumbria, that heading north from Manchester on the western side of the Pennines and that travelling northwards from

Doncaster – Ermine Street – towards York and the Northumbrian heartlands. The other branch of Ermine Street from Lincoln to the Humber crossing at Brough (*Petuaria*) was perhaps less sustainable as a military road, and if the crossing at *Petuaria* was not under strict military control, in a post-Roman world this route could be easily severed. This meant that the strategic importance of both Manchester and Doncaster during the Roman period was every bit as important, if not more so, in the post-Roman military and social landscape.

Hey notes the importance of a long-distance, north–south track which ran through South Yorkshire during the Roman period. That the routeway continued in use through the post-Roman period is suggested by it being used for parish boundaries in the Norman period (Stein, 2019, pp.4–5). It was called Ryknield Street and may have originally been a pre-Roman routeway, with all the hallmarks of a prehistoric ridgeway (Hey, 2003, pp.16–17). It crossed the River Don at a place known as Strafford Sands, close to Sprotbrough and Conisbrough. Many of its latter-day sections had 'street' names, such as East Street, Old Street, Street Lane and King's Street, the latter suggesting it continued to be maintained in the later-Saxon period as part of the apparatus of the state. Ryknield Street may well have been particularly important in a local context as it appears to have linked important pre-Conquest centres such as Morthern, Conisbrough, Barnburgh, Hooton and Adwick (Hey, 2003, p.17).

The fort at Doncaster was most likely at the head of navigation on the River Don (Buckland, 1986, p.11), and thus provided a link with the Humber and the North Sea. It was built in the first century AD and seems to have been finally abandoned in the fourth century, but probably remained as a civilian settlement thereafter; the old Roman fort of *Danum* was possibly utilized as a place of periodic refuge (*ibid.*, pp.17–18). The fort at Templeborough again dates from the first century AD and may have been abandoned earlier than Doncaster, although the evidence is sketchy. Because the area surrounding Templeborough's Roman fort has been industrialized for some considerable time, it is difficult to understand the extent of any

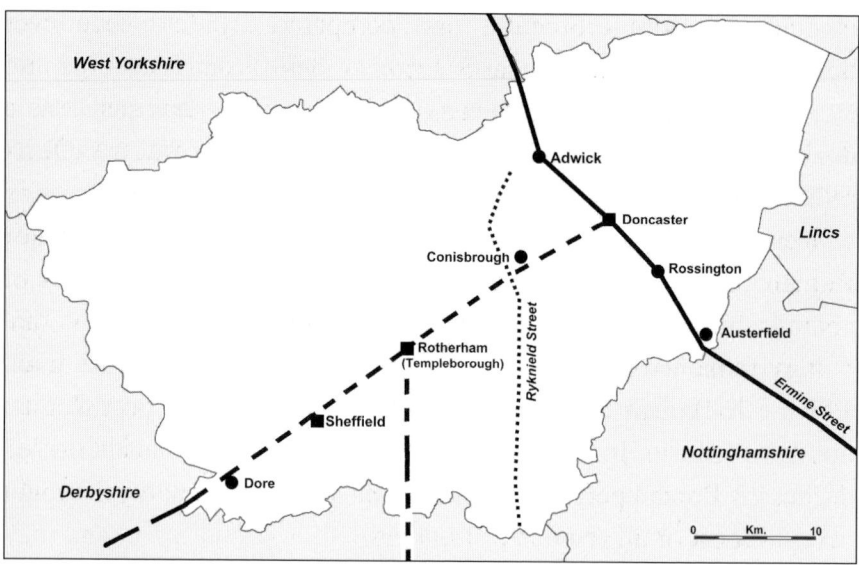

Fig. 5: Roman roads in South Yorkshire.

civilian settlement which may have surrounded the fort or whether the *vicus* outlived the military use of the facility (Buckland, 1986, p.32; Chadwick, 2019, p.7).

At Rossington Bridge, a fort has been identified on the course of Ermine Street which appears to have been part of the same consolidation by the Roman military in the first century (Chadwick, 2019, p.6). The fort probably remained in use until the late-third century and may have been a 'fall-back' or reinforcement facility for Doncaster, should the need arise. It may also have afforded protection to the large pottery industry which became established nearby. A military station has also been identified by aerial reconnaissance at Burghwallis (Buckland, 1986, p.8; Ottaway, 2019), but little is known about its lifespan (Chadwick, 2019, p.153). It may have been part of a gradual push northwards into Brigantian territory by the Roman military in the first century AD, or the appropriation and protection of Ryknield Street (see above).

Rural settlement during the Roman period, seemingly, was ubiquitous in many areas of the region, although most of the evidence is from cropmarks and comparatively few have ever been excavated. The cropmarks seem to identify late Iron Age and Romano-British rural settlements, suggesting firstly that there was a deal of continuation after the Iron Age, and secondly that the effects of Roman occupation were minimal as far as native habitation was concerned. Buckland, Magilton and Dolby note that, despite major Roman pottery kilns in the region around Rossington, the paucity of ceramic finds on native sites from the Roman period suggests that pottery remained inessential to the native tradition (Buckland et al., 1980, p.163), and this is likely to have continued in post-Roman South Yorkshire. However, it is likely that agriculture was intensified during the Roman period, and the effects of a cash economy no doubt reached most or all regions of England.

At Edlington Wood, near Doncaster, is a series of stone and earthen banks, where a Roman brooch and coin hoard were found. The settlement comprised D-shaped and sub-rectangular enclosures built of limestone blocks facing stone and earth banks, with a series of stone buildings and archaeological evidence for occupation from the late first to the early fourth century AD. The pottery, coin and metal finds indicate there was at least one relatively high-status settlement in the immediate area (Chadwick, 2019, p.19), and recent Lidar analysis indicates that the enclosures at Edlington Wood formed part of a co-axial field system of low stone banks (Buckland, Buckland and Prosser, 2017). This particular settlement was on the Magnesian Limestone ridge, while a little further south on the limestone ridge at Oldcoates, a Roman villa with a mosaic floor was excavated in 1870 (Historic England, 2020, Listed entry 1006385). It is likely that the better farmland of the limestone ridge was chosen by the more affluent and Romanized inhabitants. At Scabba Wood, near Sprotbrough, Doncaster, a walled Romano-British enclosure was also located on the Magnesian Limestone, as were earthworks identified in woodland such as at Edlington. Most enclosures on the Magnesian Limestone areas of South Yorkshire share a morphology with the so-called co-axial 'brickwork' fields to the south-east; these were rectangular or sub-rectangular in plan, whereas on the Coal Measures to the west, more sub-circular forms are found (Chadwick, 2019, pp.22–23). Outside of the limestone areas of South Yorkshire, aerial reconnaissance has been the principal identifier of settlement sites, and the preservation of Roman-period settlements in woodland on the Magnesian Limestone ridge is significant to the post-Roman occupation of the region (or lack of), and will be returned to later.

After the collapse of the Roman economy and the military withdrawal, it is likely that the large rural estates became the focus of settlement, economics and power, with what remained of the military probably focussing attention on their survival (Higham, 1993a, p.55). To what extent the Roman rural estates evolved into those of the post-Roman period is not clear, but it may have been that many of the 'multiple estates' had their origins in the Roman period. The Roman economy no doubt exploited all of the resources available, be they predominantly arable, livestock or even mineral. To some extent, the east–west orientation of the Roman road system in southern Yorkshire and northern Derbyshire was partly to protect the lead-bearing veins in the limestone of the White Peak. It is likely that the fort at *Navio* (Brough-on-Noe), in particular, was erected to safeguard Roman lead interests in the Peak District as it lies to the immediate north of the lead veins and close to the southern boundary of the Brigantes (Hart, 1981, p.83).

Despite the Roman economy being more centralized, the notion of localized ecozones was still as pertinent in Roman Britain as it was at any other time. Whilst some areas were well-suited to arable farming, where we particularly see the concentration of villa estates (Higham, 1993a, p.41), other areas were equally important in the production of, for example, livestock, timber or minerals, leading to specialized production. Perhaps the main difference was that the Roman economy intensified this specialisation in each ecozone as a consequence of the market system. The collapse of the Roman economy would have caused each area to look to itself for providing subsistence at a regional or local level, but this was probably a gradual process as

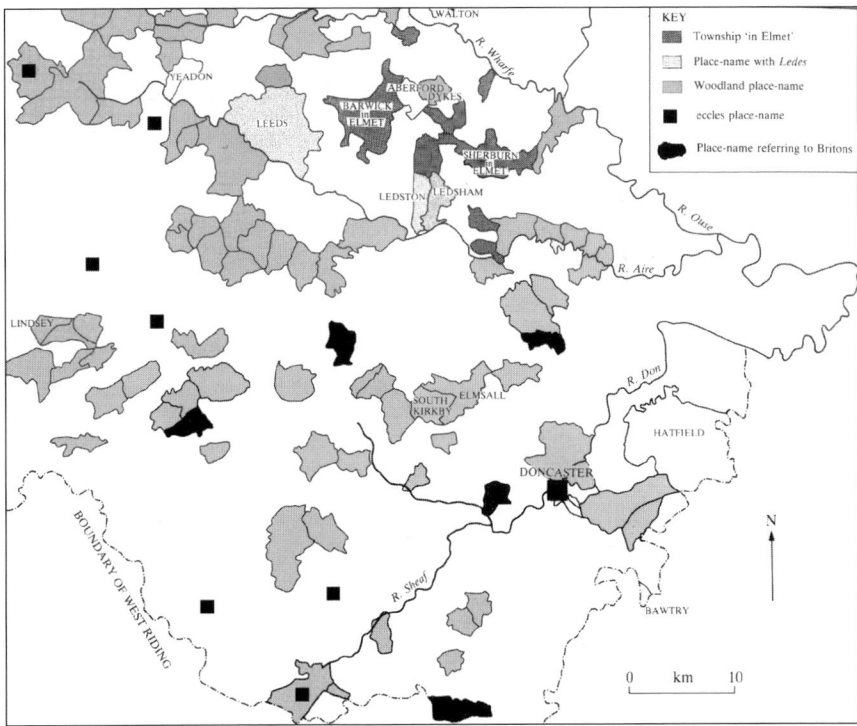

Fig. 6: Woodland in south-western Yorkshire (from Higham, 1993a).

the economy did not disintegrate overnight. However, any shortfalls in production (for example, the lack of grain in Pennine Yorkshire) may have encouraged trading with other regions. During the Roman period, deforestation was at its peak, possibly with less woodland than there is today. However, the collapse of the Roman economy resulted in the regeneration of woodland, especially in the upland areas (Higham, 1993a, p.74) and on the less productive soils. Fig. 6 shows the extent of woodland place-names in southern Yorkshire, suggesting that a large proportion of the area became wooded by the later-Saxon period.

Chapter 2

South Yorkshire in a Post-Roman Context

The early development of the region

The Roman legacy to the Anglo-Saxon period took several forms, not least that late-Roman art and architecture was adopted into the pantheon of insular Anglo-Saxon art and the reuse of Roman dressed stone certainly provided a direct legacy for early church-builders, as will be discussed later. But before that, some, if not most, of the major Roman communication routes continued through the Anglo-Saxon period (and beyond), and Roman agricultural estates probably survived into the post-Roman period, although this is still debated. However, the post-Roman period began in darkness as far as our knowledge of organisation, settlement and interaction is concerned. It was a post-Roman Iron Age, but how similar this was to that which had gone before the Roman conquest is unknown. From the fourth century AD onwards, South Yorkshire remains archaeologically and historically obscure for some considerable time. The market system in Roman Britain had given way to one of subsistence, perhaps with minimal trade between the various native groups, now faced with a largely introspective economic strategy. The nature of society in this part of England in the post-Roman period is largely unknown. It is likely that a Roman style of local government survived in certain parts, in one form or another, but to what extent and where is again unknown. The development of 'warrior elites' seems prevalent. Any continuity of settlement sites from the Roman period into the post-Roman is poorly understood, largely because there is an archaeological dearth of material culture and evidence for post-Roman burial practice.

Following the collapse of the Roman economy, environmental sampling has shown a decline in agricultural production, especially on the more marginal landscapes such as the Pennine areas. Loveluck sees this as most likely due to a reduced demand for surplus now there was no need to feed the Roman Empire (Loveluck, 2003, p.154).

It seems that leadership in many areas of eastern England passed to Germanics who became known as the Anglo-Saxons, but the process of takeover (if that is what it was) is unclear. The writings of Bede in the eighth century frequently described the people and places of eastern England, but remained largely silent when it came to western areas. Near contemporary sources – for example that compiled by the British monk Gildas – tell of wholesale murder and pillage, with the native population being put to the sword or fleeing for their lives. But these sources were written from places remote from Germanic settlement, and neither of these events appear to be true; there is no archaeological evidence to suggest either widespread 'cleansing' of the native populace or wholesale migration. As many writers have observed, it would make no sense for the Germanic incomers to drive away the indigenous population when the obvious aim would be to take control of an economy with its workforce and organisations in place.

We know that mercenary Germanic soldiers were part of the Roman army in Britain, their presence being both documented and attested to archaeologically. In the north and west, it seems several warlords emerged, stepping into the vacuum left by the Roman military, eventually forming petty tribal 'kingships'. Northumbria and Deira are British names, and even Hatfield, immediately to the east of South Yorkshire, is recorded by its British name in Welsh writings and was still known as such by the ninth century. There is little evidence that there was any Germanic presence in the North by the mid-fifth century, and even by the sixth and seventh centuries it was concentrated in the Vale of York, with almost no obvious presence in the Pennines (Higham, 1993a, pp.59–66). How Germanic people integrated with the native populace is not clear. What seems evident, especially from the archaeological record, is that Germanic settlement was selective. Some areas, for example much of Lincolnshire, East Yorkshire and the East Midlands, appear to have been target areas for the Germanics, taking control of the richer agricultural lands where the relatively light and fertile soils provided good farmland. This was in contrast with the Pennine uplands and the heavier soils of the Coal Measures sandstones found in southern Yorkshire, which seems to have been avoided as a focus for Anglo-Saxon settlement, although their economic wealth was no doubt recognized by them.

The Pennine regions are poorly documented by Bede. He made mention of 'the forest of Elmet', a district called 'Loidis' and a royal palace and church at a mysterious location known as *Campodonum*, as well as writing that there was a British king in Elmet surviving at least until the seventh century (Sherley-Price, 1955, pp.132, 245). The latter is particularly interesting in that this continuing British administration correlates with a lack of Anglo-Saxon material evidence discovered in this region, with practically no physical Germanic infiltration. Loveluck makes the point that the lack of material culture need not necessarily mean impoverishment, but rather a difference in approaches to cultural expression, perhaps through ideological methods of display (Loveluck, 2003, p.155). It is almost certain that Ceretic, the British leader of Elmet, paid tribute to the Northumbrian Saxons (if that is what they were), perhaps with a levy of slaves, livestock, wool or timber as the condition of his continued control over the region and its native people. Ceretic's jurisdiction is unknown; it seems he controlled several small land units in the region as well as Elmet, although the extent of this is a mystery (Higham, 1993a, pp.86–87; Loveluck, 2003, p.156). As well as Ceretic of Elmet, the poem *Y Gododdin* tells of several other British warriors from upland areas (Loveluck, 2003, p.156).

Apart from Loidis (assumed to refer to the Leeds area), the only other place mentioned by Bede in this region was 'Elmet Wood' and its proximity to a royal palace at *Campodonum*, a site which has not yet been identified. It has been suggested to be the Roman settlement at Slack, near Hebden Bridge in West Yorkshire, or Doncaster in South Yorkshire (Shirley-Price, 1955, p.132). Higham favours the Roman fort site at Doncaster (1993a, pp.85–86), and *Campodonum* is said by Bede to be the site where the bishop Paulinus founded a stone church; indeed, the masonry of the Roman fort there would have provided the materials (Higham, 1993a, p.112). Bede says that *Campodonum* had a royal residence which was sacked by pagans (meaning the Mercians). The stone altar from the royal basilica there survived the devastation and was said to have been taken to a monastery in the 'Forest of Elmet', wherever that may have been. Bede goes on to say that the royal seat at *Campodonum* was later replaced by one near Loidis (Shirley-Price, 1955, p.132), and given that it was sacked following an encroachment by Mercia in the seventh century, the likelihood is that *Campodonum* was located in land lost to Mercia at that time. In that case, Higham's equation between *Campodonum* and Doncaster becomes even the more plausible. *Danum* was certainly a site in a strategic location on the Roman routes from Mercia in the north Midlands, Lindsey and *Heathfelthlund* (Hatfield) in the east, and was on the main Roman road to the north (the only major north–south route east of the Pennines). Higham notes that *Campodonum* meant 'the field by the Danum', a name which he sees as echoing similar 'field' names in the vicinity, for example Hatfield and Austerfield (Higham, 1993a, p.86).

The annexation of Elmet by the Northumbrians, according to Bede, and its inclusion in the *Tribal Hidage* (see below) may have followed the 'Battle of the River Idle' in 616, which Hey (1979, p.20) places on the east bank of the river and which was, according to Bede, inside Mercian territory (Hey, 2003, p.25). Higham suggests this may have been near Scaftworth by the Roman road from Littleborough to Doncaster (Higham, 1993a, p.113). Interestingly, there is a 'Roman Ridge Dyke' on the east bank of the Idle at Scaftworth, which may have been a Mercian defence of the river crossing into Hatfield (ibid., p.144). The battle was fought between the Bernician king, Aethelfrith, and Raedwald of East Anglia, who was supported by Edwin of Deira (an area centred on the Vale of York), who had been in exile in East Anglia. The battle resulted in Edwin gaining control over all of Northumbria. Edwin's success continued and he extended his control to become the overlord of Lindsey. An interesting passage by Bede for the year 628 tells how King Edwin and bishop Paulinus performed a mass baptism in the River Trent on the border of Lindsey. No doubt this was a public ceremony conducted after gaining the submission of Lindsey. Bede says that this was close to the 'city' that the Anglo-Saxons called *Tiowulfingacaestir*, which remains unidentified. A 'city' was a term given by Bede for a former Roman fortified place, and given that Edwin most likely travelled to the Lindsey border southwards through Doncaster and along the Roman road known now as Till Bridge Lane, the most likely 'city' referred to here would have been *Segelocum* (Littleborough) by the west bank of the Trent (Higham, 1997, p.175). Bede goes on to say how peaceful this area had become since Edwin was in control (Sherley-Price, 1955, p.134), which suggests that previously it had been anything but tranquil; this peace, however, was not destined to last for long.

The British king, Ceretic, was said to have controlled Elmet (and possibly other areas as well) until the seventh century, when he was expelled by Edwin (Sherley-Price, 1955, p.140). This has led to the assumption that British rule in Elmet was extinguished by Northumbria's actions during the early seventh century. However, Edwin was defeated and killed in 633, at the hands of the British leader, Cadwalla, with Mercian support (Sherley-Price, 1955, p.140), which is highly likely to have resurrected the British leadership in Elmet. Cadwalla is generally taken as a British leader based in Gwynedd, although Woolf (2004) has suggested that he may have been based elsewhere. It is argued that the Welsh of Gwynedd had dynastic ties with Elmet (Kirby, 1977, p.34), and the expulsion of Ceretic (along with hostilities over the Cheshire Plain) probably added inducements to the eventual invasion of Northumbria by Cadwalla. What is particularly interesting in this respect is that a pre-Conquest inscribed stone pillar in Gwynedd bears an inscription that refers to Aliortus the Elmetian (Taylor, 1992, p.111), which will be returned to later. The stylistic date assigned to the inscribed stone is mid- to late-fifth century. This, together with the numerous 'eccles' names in the region, leads Loveluck (2003, p.156) to suggest that Elmet was established by the fifth century. However, there are dangers with stylistic dating, as well as place-name interpretation – both of which will be discussed later – so this date must be treated cautiously. How long an autonomous native administration lasted in Elmet after the victory by Cadwalla and the possible consequent resurrection of Ceretic's rule is unknown, but it may have been short-lived as we hear no more about it, although archaeological evidence tells us that Anglo-Saxon settlement in Elmet remained absent long into the nominal Saxon period.

The defeat of Edwin took place at the Battle of *Haethfelth* (Hatfield). Cadwalla's success was due largely to support from the emerging power in the western Midlands – Mercia – which soon became the main adversary to Northumbria's extensive and expansive kingdom. Mercian power continued to grow over the next two decades. Hatfield, a small political unit, was a buffer between the kingdom of Lindsey (now in northern Lincolnshire) and Elmet in southern Yorkshire. Unlike Elmet, Lindsey was subject to Germanic settlement from the mid-fifth century, if not earlier. It is likely that a British administration remained there after the collapse of Roman rule, infiltrated by Germanics either as supporters or controllers of the administration, but by the seventh century Lindsey seems to have been subordinate to either the Mercians or the Northumbrians, depending on which neighbouring power was in the ascendancy (see, for example, Sawyer, 1998).

The location of the Battle of Hatfield is unknown. Sawyer points out that the district or polity of Hatfield once extended as far south as Nottinghamshire and suggests the battle may have taken place close to Edwinstowe (Sawyer, 1998, p.57), and possibly at Cuckney some 6km away, where an undated mass burial pit was once identified (Hey, 1979, p.20). This evidence is at best tentative, if not unlikely, and the most probable location for the battle is further to the north, close to the Roman road from Lincoln to Doncaster which crossed the River Trent at or near Littleborough (*Segelocum*). As already noted, massed armies took advantage of existing Roman roads – which were well-known routes – and strategic sites such as abandoned Roman fortifications (for example those at Scaftworth and Littleborough). The Roman road near the suggested battlefield, easily traceable for much of its route today as Till Bridge Lane, passed from Lindsey through *Haethfelthlund* and approached Northumbrian lands to the north, passing through Doncaster. The last recorded battle between Mercia and Northumbria in this region was the Battle of the Trent in 679. Bede writes that 'a great battle' was fought between Egfrid of Northumbria and Ethelred of Mercia 'near the river Trent' (Sherley-Price, 1955, p.240), where the Mercians were victorious, seemingly heralding a period of relative peace between the two kingdoms, with Mercia exerting control over Lindsey. The location of this battle is unknown; 'near the River Trent' could have meant anywhere between Lincoln and *Heathfelthlund*, but it was most likely close to the old Roman forts at Littleborough or Scaftworth.

Interestingly, the route chosen by the Mercians for this battle – as with their support from northern Wales in the two earlier battles – was again through or leading towards *Haethfelthlund*, which meant that the armies must have amassed in and proceeded from Lindsey, rather than directly from the Mercian heartlands around the Vale of Trent. One possible reason for this is that the Roman road through Chesterfield from Derby to the fort at Templeborough had become impassable by the seventh century as it passed through a landscape containing a large extent of regenerated woodland. The Coal Measures sandstone area (now in north-east Derbyshire) seems to have been one of extensive forest developed as the result of regeneration after the collapse of the Roman economy (see Rackham, 1986, pp.75–83). Evidence for this is also found in the numerous place-name elements found in the Coal Measures region which refer to woodland; Elmton and Ashover are prime examples. There are also place-names

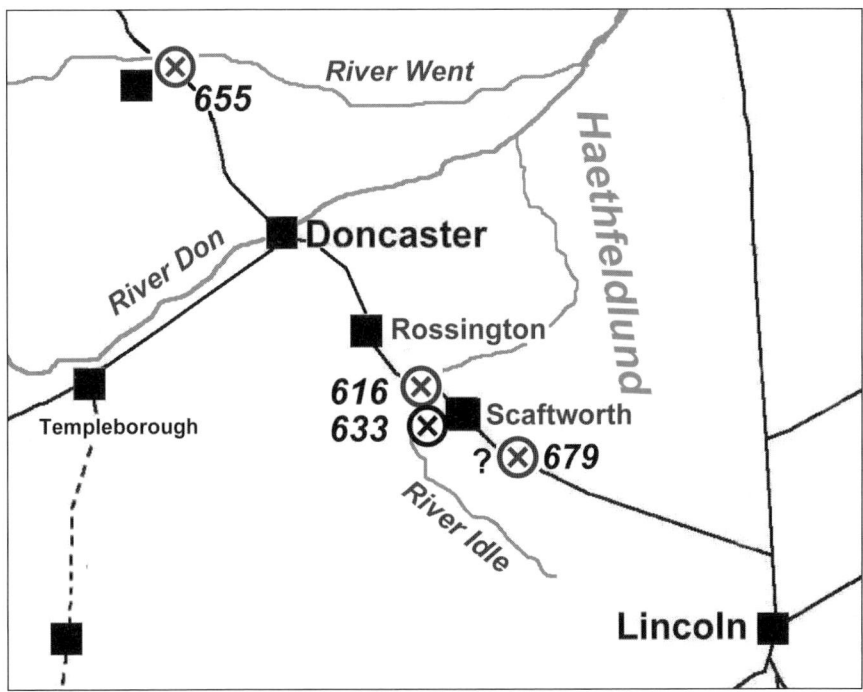

Fig. 7: Probable sites of the seventh-century battles.

suggesting poor agricultural land, such as Heath, Clay Lane and Brackenfield (Fellows-Jensen, 1978, p.257). The only other plausible route would have taken the armies through the Peak to the Roman fort at *Navio* (Bradwell-on-Noe), an area controlled by the *Pecsaetna* and probably too sensitive to risk being alienated.

Haethfelthlund survives today only in a place-name (Hatfield) and as areas known as Hatfield Woodhouse, Hatfield Moors and Hatfield Chase. Little is known about this territory, which does not seem to have been the focus of any recent research. As mentioned above, it possibly extended from the head of the Humber estuary southwards into present-day Nottinghamshire. Its western boundary appears to have been an ill-defined region of marshland and often swollen rivers around the courses of the Idle and Ryton, which did not present any suitable crossing point until higher ground was encountered, travelling southwards, immediately to the north of Everton in Nottinghamshire and where the Roman road from Littleborough into Lindsey took advantage of this (Sidebottom, 2015, pp.7–8). How much further *Haethfelthlund* extended to the south of this is unknown, but it might have been somewhere in the region of present-day Retford, although this is purely conjecture. The eastern boundary of *Haethfelthlund* may well have been the River Trent, a substantial natural boundary which became the Nottinghamshire–Lincolnshire border in later times. Archaeologically, the Trent also appears to form the limit of 'pagan' Anglo-Saxon burials (arguably those up to the mid-seventh century), which are almost all found to the east of the river in Lindsey; the distribution seems to respect a political boundary (see Campbell, 1991) and this may reflect the eastern border of *Heathfelthlund*.

Haethfelthlund is mentioned in the *Tribal Hidage* (see below), and by the time that this document was composed it was associated with Lindsey, its neighbour to the east; both seem to have been subject to

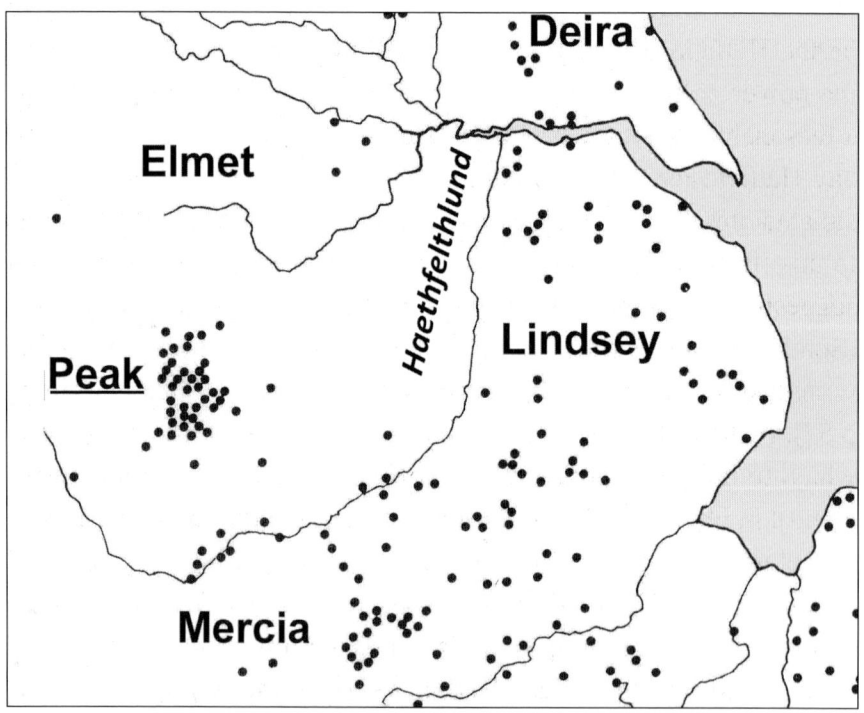

Fig. 8. *Heathfelthlund* with distribution of 7th-century burial evidence (based on Campbell 1991).

Mercian control at the time. It is possible, given that *Haethfelthlund* was largely a region of fen and marsh, that it originally comprised a series of small 'island' groups of people, including those of the Isle of Axholme, occupying areas of dry ground between the less hospitable extents of fen, each bounded together by a common economic landscape. Similar arrangements have been suggested for groups in the Lincolnshire fens, for example the *Bilmiga* or the *Spalda* (see Hart, 1977). Hatfield has always been seen as 'marginal', even when the shires were developed in the post-Viking period, and cropmarks of field systems identified from the air are similar to those of the late Iron Age which were typical of fen habitats (Higham, 1993a, p.89).

In 680, the 'Council of Hatfield' brought together Ecgfrith of Northumbria, Ethelfrith of Mercia, Aldwulf of the East Angles and Hlothere of Kent, all presided over by Archbishop Theodore (Sherley-Price, 1955, p.232). The location of this Hatfield is often taken as that now in Hertfordshire, but Higham suggests it is more likely to be the Hatfield on the Lindsey and South Yorkshire borders, given the power politics at the time (Higham, 1993a, p.89), which seems a reasonable assertion. The royal centre might have been at present-day Hatfield itself (*ibid.*), possibly because it was on a 'fen island' situated close to the Northumbrian border. Interestingly, Bede refers to this 'Hatfield' as going by the English version of its name (ibid.), suggesting that it may have had a British alternative. Indeed, Hatfield (South Yorkshire) was still recorded as a separate polity by Welsh writers in the ninth century, using its British name of 'Meicen' (ibid., p.59). Perhaps it was seen as relatively neutral or contested ground on which to hold the council; *Haethfelthlund* was under Northumbrian control in 680, but subject to Mercian rule by 685 (ibid., pp.80, 88).

Returning to the contested lands between Mercia and Northumbria, the Battle of Winwaed in 655 was seemingly decisive for the Northumbrians, defeating not only Penda of Mercia but also his Welsh support and that from East Anglia. Although the River Winwaed is not located by Bede, it is generally held to be the River Went to the north of Doncaster. Bede describes it as swollen by heavy rain at the time, having flooded its surroundings (Sherley-Price, 1955, p.184); this was probably on the flat lands on or near the Roman road to the west of Wentbridge, now in West Yorkshire. If this was so, this foiled attack from Mercia was well into land to the north of South Yorkshire, suggesting that the principal defensible site in South Yorkshire, Doncaster, was already in Mercian hands.

The material evidence for a Germanic presence in southern Yorkshire

Post-Roman burial evidence in southern Yorkshire remains elusive, apparently largely due to an inability to identify anything separate from that which went before. At Parlington Hollins, near Barwick-in-Elmet, a number of interments were discovered in the 1990s which were thought to be from the late-Iron Age and Roman periods, according to the form of burial rites in evidence. However, radiocarbon dates have subsequently shown that these burials were a mix of late and post-Roman inhumations, the latter dated to the fifth or sixth centuries (possibly even the seventh), including a decapitated inhumation with hobnails which again was previously thought to be earlier than it was (Roberts, 2018, p.185). Similarly, two crouched burials found by the A1 at Ferrybridge in 2002, were radiocarbon dated to between the fifth and seventh centuries, despite being found alongside first- or second-century pottery. At Wattle Syke, near Collingham in West Yorkshire, a flexed burial was radiocarbon dated to the seventh century, and appears to have taken place in a former Roman settlement (*ibid.*, pp.185–86).

Although this relatively new evidence is limited, it certainly outlines the probability that society in southern Yorkshire in the post-Roman period was little different from that of late Roman times, which in turn had continued many late Iron-Age traditions. It also suggests, particularly from the Ferrybridge example, that society was largely aceramic. The implications are that there is much more Dark Age evidence from southern Yorkshire which has been wrongly assigned to an earlier period, lacking, as it did, an Anglo-Saxon material culture. Roberts (2018) has recently reviewed the archaeological evidence for 'Elmet' and came to this same conclusion, citing the reinterpretation of some artefacts that were previously presumed to be from the Roman period, but were re-evaluated to the earlier centuries of the post-Roman period. Another probable reason for the lack of material culture, which is normally associated with the 'British' post-Roman period, is that it is unlikely that post-Roman continental goods made their way as far north as southern Yorkshire (*ibid.*, p.190).

Despite southern Yorkshire being a focus for the rivalry between Mercia and Northumbria, there is surprisingly little archaeological evidence for an identifiable Anglo-Saxon presence in the region. What evidence does exist suggests a Germanic presence only in the east of the region, focussing on potentially strategic locations. This seems to have been the case throughout both present-day South and West Yorkshire. Faull and Moorhouse (1981, p.179) note how little Anglo-Saxon material culture can be identified in West Yorkshire, comprising little more than a couple of brooches and a few beads from the sixth or seventh centuries. In the east of West Yorkshire, some evidence has recently come to light to suggest settlement by either Germanic immigrants or natives adopting a Germanic culture. At Parlington Hollins, two sunken buildings – often known as *grubenhauser* – were discovered and their fills were dated to the post-Roman period. One contained typically Romano-British finds, but the other had over 100 sherds of Anglo-Saxon pottery (Roberts, 2018, p.187). *Grubenhauser* structures are well-known 'ethnically' Germanic buildings found in England and on the continent, and these examples found close to Ermine Street in southern Yorkshire suggest that there was some interface here between the local native society and the Anglo-Saxons.

Germanic burial evidence is equally sparse. In 1981, Faull and Moorhouse cited just four pre-Christian burials in West Yorkshire that can be identified as 'Anglo-Saxon' (1981, 179-180). One was located at Dalton Parlours (Collingham) found with a broach and pottery at the site of a Roman villa. Another burial was discovered at Pontefract in 1855 with a spindle whorl and iron ladle; in 1962 a male burial with a spearhead and seventh-century buckle at North Elmsall; at Ferry Fryston a barrow burial was excavated 1863 with 4 secondary inhumations, one with 'armour', a spear and a sword. In 1856 a crouched burial was discovered at Leeds, close to the River Aire, which may have been Anglo-Saxon but this is uncertain (*ibid.*) and now largely discredited (Roberts 2018, 184). At the time of writing, further burial evidence in the region was emerging from Garforth. Here, a lead coffin had been discovered which contained what was described as the remains of a high-status Roman woman in a cemetery that otherwise contained both 'Roman' graves in a roughly east-west alignment and 'Saxon' graves with a north-south alignment (BBC News, March 13th, 2023). The cemetery appears to date to the early-fifth century and seemingly shows two cultures co-existing well together. It is tempting to speculate that the Anglo-Saxon presence here, at such a relatively-early date, could represent mercenary support for a local native elite. No doubt further reporting will follow as analysis from this site continues.

If the uncertain Anglo-Saxon burial near Leeds is discounted, all of the Anglo-Saxon burial evidence is from the east of West Yorkshire, in particular flanking the Roman road of Ermine Street, which in turn follows the Magnesian Limestone ridge (see Fig. 9). In South Yorkshire, an Anglo-Saxon cemetery was discovered at Adwick-le-Street in 2007 with thirty-seven *in situ* burials and a limited number of grave goods. Isotope analysis of seven individuals showed mixed origins, including local, regional or national migrants and two long-distance migrants (McKinley, 2016, p.77). With one exception, the graves all followed the same general north-east–south-west alignment and comprised male and female burials, with more than one child (the majority were female). The combined radiocarbon, artefactual and contextual evidence points to a late seventh- to mid to late eighth-century date for the cemetery (ibid., p.89). A mixed-rite, Romano-British cemetery was discovered in the 1960s some 200–300 metres to the north-west (Buckland and Magilton, 1986, pp.214–20). In 2001, the remains of a ninth-century

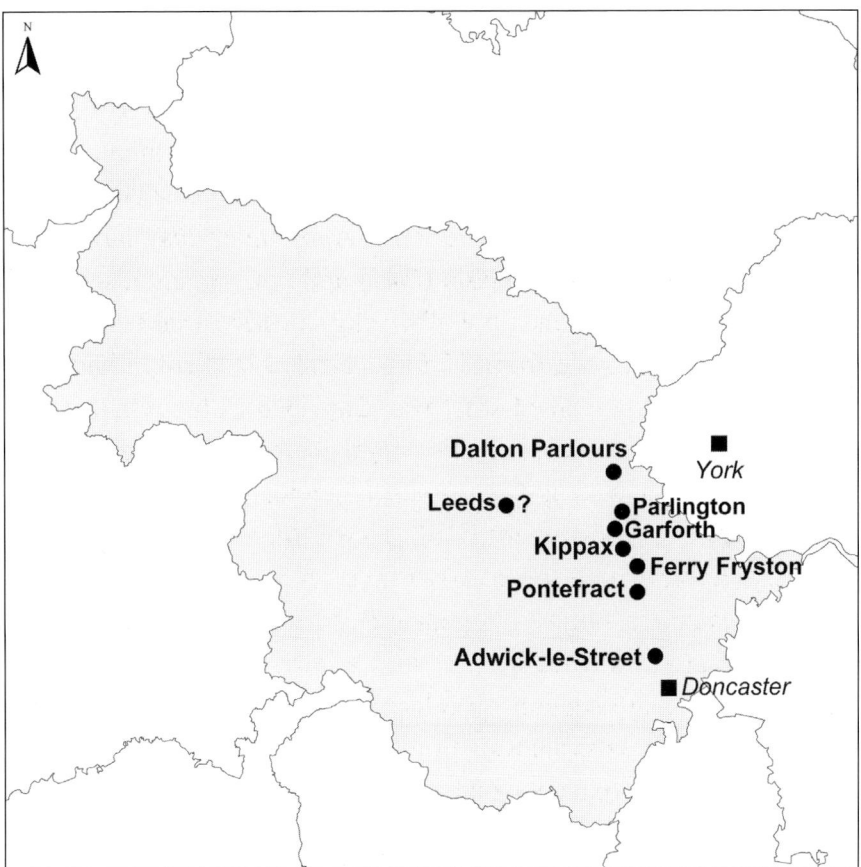

Fig. 9: Anglo-Saxon burial and *Grubenhauser* evidence in the former West Riding.

Viking inhumation burial (adult female) were recovered from a grave that cut through a Romano-British ditch a little further to the north-west of the site (Speed and Walton Rogers, 2004).

Adwick-le-Street lies on the Roman road just to the north of Doncaster. The alignment of the grave rows is almost parallel with the road and perpendicular to a possible Roman trackway to the north. The road, however, follows the crest of the ridge, and the fall of the land is likely to have been the major influence on the positioning of the grave rows. Proximity to the road, and possibly more importantly the Romano-British cemetery to the north, may have been factors in the cemetery location. The size of the earlier cemetery is unclear,

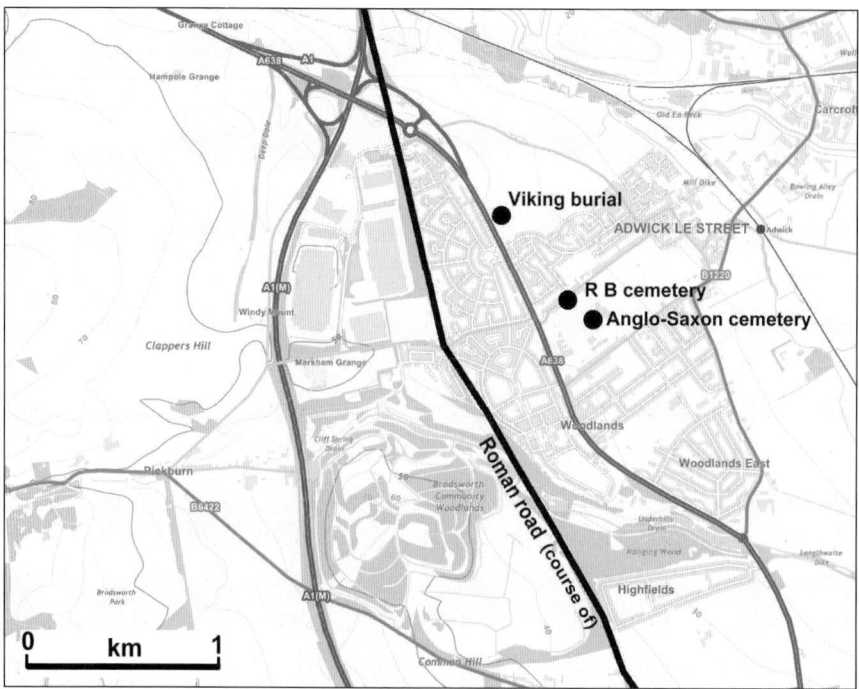

Fig. 10: Anglo-Saxon and Viking burial evidence in South Yorkshire (Opendata map).

but both it and the road are likely to have at least been known to exist, if not directly visible, in the late-seventh century. The attraction of earlier burial sites (and other structures) as an appropriate place for their own dead is well documented for the early Anglo-Saxons, but the reuse of Roman sites had become rare by the seventh century (McKinley, 2016, p.107). However, as discussed above, this was not just the reuse of a Roman-period burial site, but the reuse of Doncaster itself and its environs as a strategic centre in the post-Roman period.

The cemetery at Adwick-le-Street is quite a rarity in South Yorkshire. Pre-Conquest burial remains have been found in churchyard locations at Conisbrough and Hickleton, about 9km to the south and south-west of the site, but these are from a much later date than the cemetery at Adwick (McKinley, 2016) and followed the nucleation of settlement and the reorganization of the political landscape during the later Saxon period, as will be discussed later. It is notable that no burials from the post-Roman period have ever been found south of the River

30

Don in South Yorkshire or from north-east Derbyshire (Roberts, 2018; Barrett, 2000), the most likely reason for which is explained later in the discussion. An examination of artefacts recovered from South Yorkshire and dating to the Anglo-Saxon period is quite illuminating; they are all found in locations which strongly suggest that Anglo-Saxon infiltration in South Yorkshire was limited. Possible Saxon pottery was found at Adwick-le-Street, and eleven sherds of Torksey-type ware and two sherds of York A-type ware with a small quantity – maybe three or four sherds – of a possible pre-Conquest gritty ware were found at Arksey, just to the north of Doncaster (Cumberpatch, 2016). A bronze ingot, which may be Anglo-Saxon, was discovered at Hatfield in 1976 (South Yorkshire Sites & Monuments Record/SMR), while evidence from the Portable Antiquities Scheme again shows that Anglo-Saxon incursions were taking place only along the eastern border of Elmet, principally along the Magnesian Limestone (Roberts, 2018, p.189), where the Roman road, Ermine Street, provided a corridor between the emerging kingdoms. However, apart from post-Roman evidence at Doncaster – discussed below – artefactual evidence from the period has also been discovered at Conisbrough and its neighbour, Cadeby, on the opposite side of the River Don.

The evidence from Conisbrough is interesting. Running north-west from St Peter's Church is Wellgate, where an excavation in 2002 revealed a plank-walled construction which was dated by dendrochronology to the late-sixth and early-seventh centuries. This may have formed part of a stock pond for fish, associated with an elite residence close to the surviving Anglo-Saxon church and a nearby well (Buckland, Hey, O'Neill and Tyers, 2013) which probably provided a local water supply. To the south of Conisbrough, a Roman 'villa' has been identified and the Wellgate site was probably located within the Roman estate attached to the villa (ibid., p.3). The excavation failed to reveal any artefactual evidence other than residual Roman pottery, and therefore it is unclear whether this structure was part of an Anglo-Saxon facility or one which was post-Roman native. However, what it does show is that Conisbrough was certainly occupied during the post-Roman period, raising the possibility that there was a continuum of localized control here from the Roman period; a location of strategic importance, overlooking the crossing of the River Don by the routeway, Ryknield Street. The evidence is strengthened by the recovery, over the years, of three sherds of Torksey ware and a total of eighteen sherds of various Lincolnshire wares spanning the period between the mid-fifth and early-eleventh centuries, all found at Conisbrough Castle (Cumberpatch, 2016). A charter dating to 664 records a large number of landholdings ceded to the abbey at Peterborough, known then as *Medeshamstede*, by King Wulfhere of Mercia. Most of these parcels of land were in the eastern Midlands, but the charter also included three Yorkshire estates, one of which is described as at Conisbrough (*Cuningesburge*) (Sawyer charter S68). The charter may, however, have been an eleventh-century forgery or possibly a 'rewrite', but one can reasonably assume that Conisbrough may have been a viable estate by the mid-seventh century. The importance of Conisbrough is discussed further below.

Further evidence of a continued post-Roman occupation comes from Goldthorpe in South Yorkshire, which is located just to the north of Bolton-upon-Dearne and Barnburgh, about 7 or 8km north-west of Conisbrough. Archaeological investigations in 2013 revealed that there was a continuum of the Roman field system, at least in part, and the continued use of 'Roman' corn drying ovens, the latest dated between the fourth and sixth centuries AD (Ross et al., 2017). The archaeological evidence supports the idea that the economy of southern Pennine Yorkshire was perhaps affected less by the collapse of the Roman economy than many other areas, and is a reflection on the level of Romanization – or rather the lack of it – which enabled the economy of the region to survive, albeit in a modified form. Perhaps it would be fair to say that most of the people of the southern Pennines actually prospered from being largely left alone, firstly by the Romans and then, as we shall see, by the Germanics and Scandinavians who followed them. It is interesting that the ovens and field system at Goldthorpe, close to Barnburgh and Bolton-upon-

Dearne, are located in an area that seems to have been important in the post-Roman period, as will be discussed further below.

At Pot Ridings Wood in the parish of Cadeby, approximately 2km north-east of Conisbrough, further finds are known from the Anglo-Saxon period. Here, the evidence is artefactual, found largely through metal detecting. It includes three bronze buckles, a bronze pin and two sherds of possible Anglo-Saxon pottery, the latter most likely imported into the area rather than produced locally. Dateable evidence comes in the form of a styca coin of Aedelred II of Northumbria (*c.* 841–84) and a ninth-century strap end (South Yorkshire SMR). The dateable finds from the ninth century may relate to the eve of the Viking invasions, or alternatively could be portable wealth seized by the latter. For South Yorkshire, the number of casual Anglo-Saxon finds from Cadeby suggests that it was some form of settlement, but we are not able to say more than this. Notably, the name 'Cadeby' is indicative of an early Scandinavian settlement, one in a pattern of similar place-names, as discussed below. Pot Ridings Wood stands just above the north bank of the River Don in an area subject to extensive limestone quarrying, and it is almost certain that much evidence has been lost. The River Don passes along a gorge through the Magnesian Limestone ridge at this point, and although Doncaster was probably the head of navigation for most river traffic, it is quite feasible that more shallow-draught vessels could proceed through the gorge as far as Conisbrough. Cadeby overlooks the shallows passing through the gorge. On the opposite side of the river stands the highest point in the local area, Butterbusk. The South Yorkshire SMR records earthworks here and an indication of stone buildings in a field north-east of Butterbusk Farm, with a tradition of a connection with Conisborough Castle. The nature of Butterbusk's past is as yet unknown, but it stands within sight of both Doncaster and Conisbrough and may, therefore, have been a significant point in the early-medieval landscape.

It can be seen that the distribution of artefacts that identify a Germanic material culture in South Yorkshire is limited to the east of the county, appearing to be particularly focussed on communication

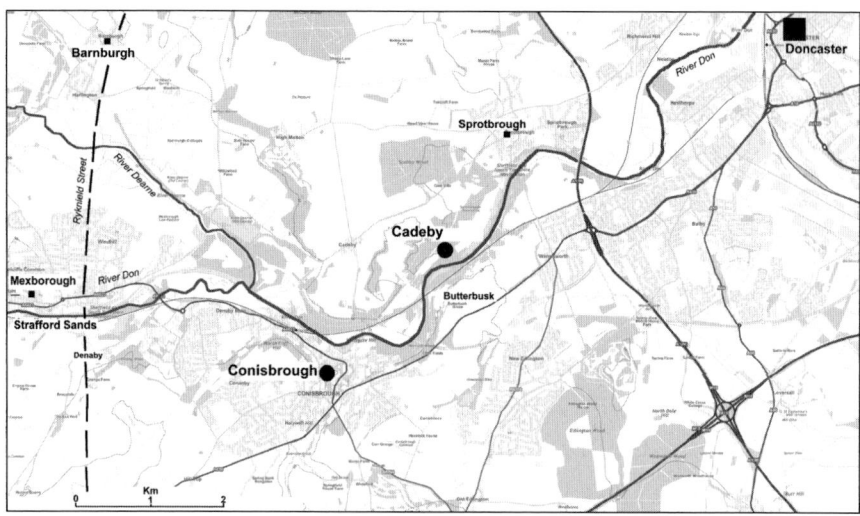

Fig. 11: Cadeby and Conisbrough (Opendata map).

routes: firstly, the navigable section of the River Don, which appears to have enabled Anglo-Saxon incursions perhaps as far as Conisbrough, and secondly, the Roman road, Ermine Street, where it crosses the river at the former fortified Roman site at Doncaster. This suggests a largely military-based Anglo-Saxon domination of the region, from a base or bases with good communications from outside the area. Given the seemingly restricted nature of an Anglo-Saxon presence in South Yorkshire, this argues for a continuing ethnically-British region, most likely providing tribute to Anglo-Saxon overlords who exercised control from their prime settlements in areas such as the Vale of York or the Midlands. The lack of material culture, especially pottery, suggests that it became aceramic after the collapse of the Roman economy (see Cumberpatch, 2011), making the detection of Dark Age South Yorkshire even more problematic.

Chapter 3

The *Tribal Hidage* and the Formation of the Large Kingdoms

The *Tribal Hidage* was a list of separate groups of people in southern England and the Midlands for which economic values, measured in hides, were allocated to each. It appears in several manuscripts, copied from an older document, the earliest surviving copy dating to the eleventh century (Recension A) (Davies and Vierck, 1974, pp.224–25). The general consensus is that the original may have been written sometime between the seventh and ninth centuries, although opinions differ as to exactly when (Featherstone, 2001). Whatever date it was written, it postdates the rise of Mercia as a significant political power and was drafted before the Viking settlement of the ninth century. The *Tribal Hidage* appears to be a list compiled by the controlling power of various groups from whom tribute (payment in kind) was demanded, but since the document was anonymous, we are unsure for whose benefit it was compiled. It is also not entirely clear what the status would have been of the groups mentioned in the *Tribal Hidage*. Burch suggests they should be regarded as 'kingdoms', since, *inter alia*, the *Elmedsaetna* – Elmet – is noted by Bede to have had a 'king'. However, the notion of 'kingship' may have been a construct of the rulers of the larger units, such as Northumbria, and otherwise the leaders of the groups may not have thought of themselves in this way.

The general consensus is that the *Tribal Hidage* was a Mercian document, as the groups mentioned seem to have been firmly within the sphere of Greater Mercia and it includes detailed knowledge about even the smallest of units which comprised the Mercian kingdom. Some, however, have argued that it may have been a Northumbrian account listing all the Mercian groups over whom it acted as overlord during a period of its supremacy (Brooks, 1989; Higham, 1993a, pp.115–18). It is true to say that the *Tribal Hidage* does appear to have included some lands that were at one time under the control of Northumbria, especially the *Elmedsaetna*, Lindsey and *Haethfelthlund*, but equally there were times that Mercia, too, exerted control over the same contentious land units, sandwiched as they were between the two kingdoms. There are three documented instances, both in the middle of the seventh century, which could have resulted in either kingdom becoming dominant over the other and consequently annexing the buffer states between the two. One of these is the defeat and death of Edwin of Northumbria at the hands of Cadwalla and Penda, which resulted in Mercia extending its authority to the north, which is highly likely to have included Elmet and Hatfield. Northumbria, on the other hand, could have nominally become the overlord of Mercia (and thus demanded tribute from its component parts) after the success of Oswy at the Battle of Winwaed in 655, extending its authority due to the demise of Mercia's powerful king Penda. As a mark of the volatility of the seventh century, a time when the larger kingdoms were struggling for supremacy and power, another Mercian advantage presented itself through its king Wulfhere and his successors less than ten years later when Northumbrian authority was overturned and territory previously lost was recovered. That the *Tribal Hidage* refers to 'original Mercia' as its first entry suggests that it was not written until after Wulfhere regained this territory from the Northumbrians in 657, and was probably compiled as a result of Wulfhere's expanding dominance over other groups immediately thereafter.

These accounts of the ebbing and flowing of power between Mercia and Northumbria are all related to us by the writings of Bede in the early-eighth century (see Sherley-Price, 1955). After this, there is no contemporary document that chronicles the power struggles between the two kingdoms. By the time that the *Anglo-Saxon Chronicles* were first written, most likely in the late-ninth century, the focus was on the West Saxons and their warring relationships with the various Viking groups; both Mercia and Northumbria had become subject to Viking conquests by then and the political map of Britain had changed significantly. The lack of historical documentation for the mid-Saxon period makes the *Tribal Hidage* both enigmatic and intriguing. It contains no geographical indicators to enable territorial extents to be reconstructed, although many of the groups mentioned can be located to topographical areas or through other forms of evidence such as place-names. The compilation of the *Hidage* also incorporates a clockwise, or 'sunwise', order which spirals the names of the land units around the first entry, 'original Mercia' – the old Mercian heartlands – which at least enables some geographical positioning to be made.

Despite the *Tribal Hidage* existing only as a list of people groups (see Fig. 12), some reconstruction of their geographical territories can

Myrcna lands	30,000	Hwinca	7,000
Wocansaetna	7,000	Cilternsaetna	4,000
Westerna	7,000	Hendrica	3,500
Pecsaetna	1,200	Unccung-ga	1,200
Elmedsaetna	**600**	Arosaetna	600
Lindesfarona with Heathfelthlund	7,000	Faerpinga	300
South Gyrwa	600	Bilmigga	600
North Gyrwa	600	Widerigga	600
East Wixna	300	East Willa	600
West Wixna	600	West Willa	600
Spalda	600	East Engle	30,000
Wigesta	900	East Sexena	7,000
Herefinna	1,200	Cantwarena	15,000
Sweordora	300	Suth Sexna	7,000
Gifla	300	West Sexna	100,000
Hicca	300		-----------
Wihtgara	600		
Noxgaga	6,000	Addition in manuscript	242,700
Ohtgaga	2,000		----------
		Recte	244,100
Addition in manuscript	66,100		

Fig. 12: Tribal Hidage list (after Higham, 1993a).

be attempted (Hart, 1977; Brooks, 1989, pp.160, 275). How successful any reconstruction might be, however, is debateable. Some take the view that territorial limits were too ill-defined to reconcile with strict geographical areas (see Brooks, 1989, p.160), but others regard the small groups as geographically coherent in that they appear to have operated within well-defined geographical regions (Bassett, 1989, p.21). Hart (1977, p.45) admits that the reconstruction of hard-and-fast boundaries is improbable, but it seems likely that even if the boundaries were once fluid, eventually all the groups listed in the *Hidage* must have given regard to some form of territorial geography (Higham, 1993a, p.81), especially to controlling powers who wished to quantify the extent of their activities. The writer's reconstruction of the land unit of the *Pecsaetna* (Sidebottom, 2020) identifies this with a geological and topographical identity, a group firmly attached to the limestone region of the Peak District, people operating within a common landscape and economic unit. Similar comments may well apply to other groups mentioned in the *Hidage* who found an affinity in working a similar economic landscape. The smaller groups listed in the *Hidage* may well represent the fundamental building blocks from which all the historic kingdoms were constructed (Higham and Ryan, 2013, p.139).

A reconstruction of likely physical boundaries recreated from the *Tribal Hidage* is given in Fig. 13. This is largely that put forward by Hart (1977), but includes minor modification in the light of more recent evidence (Sidebottom, 2020, pp.19–21). One particular criticism which can be levied at many reconstructions of Anglo-Saxon period land divisions – and this includes Hart's work on the *Tribal Hidage* – is that later shire boundaries have sometimes been used as lines of demarcation to compensate for the lack of geographical information from contemporary historical sources. Whilst this might be tenable, especially in some southern areas, in the north Midlands and southern Yorkshire, shire boundaries are not relevant until the very late Anglo-Saxon period since they did not reflect the bounds of former land units. Gelling argues that shire boundaries in the north Midlands did

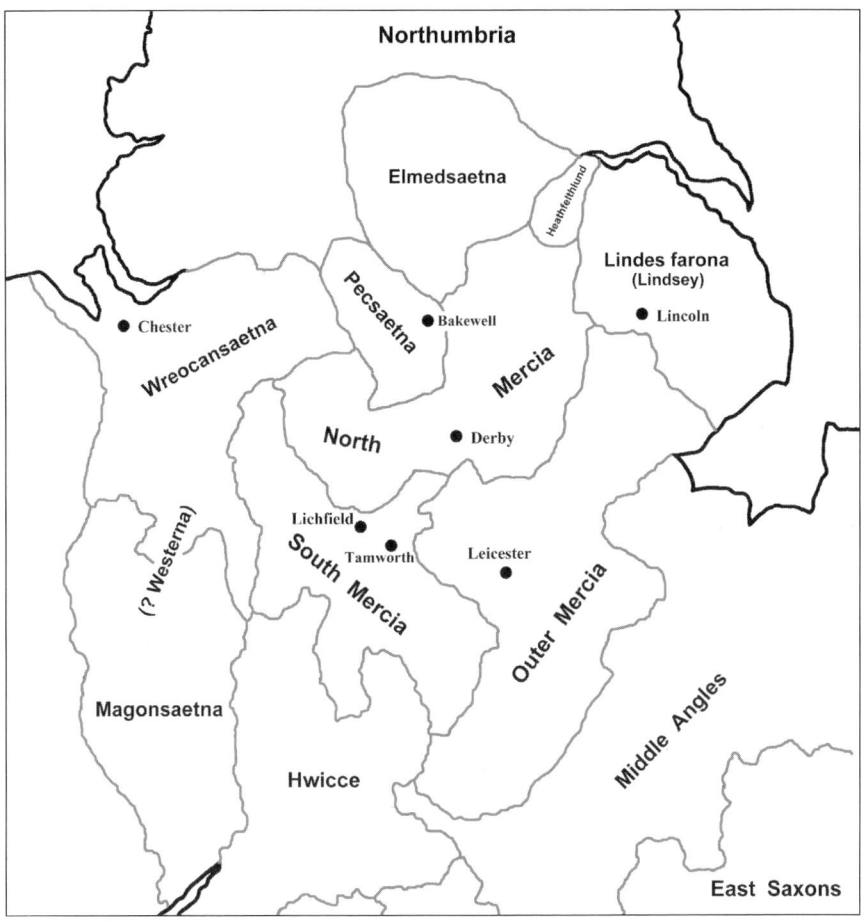

Fig. 13: Tribal Hidage map, based on Hart, 1977.

not follow pre-existing land divisions in this region as a deliberate policy and were essentially created from nothing by the West Saxons to destroy the cohesion of local groups (Gelling, 1992, pp.141–42). So we can reasonably surmise that the *Tribal Hidage* was compiled somewhere around *c.* 660, certainly before the Viking incursions of the mid-ninth century. During these 200 years, there would have been opportunities for territorial boundary changes, but for some of the land units – especially those which periodically became political buffers between the kingdoms – major territorial reorganisation was unlikely. Those units which appear to have been defined by specific ecozones are even less likely to have seen significant change taking place. Politically, too, territorial fluidity is less likely where some form of semi-independent administration was involved, and this appears to have been the case with the *Elmedsaetna* if not with other buffer states in the region.

The *Elmedsaetna* and their neighbours to the south, the *Pecsaetna*, did not have rigid and permanent attachments to either Mercia or Northumbria. As units wedged between the two kingdoms, they were subject to changing loyalties as Mercia and Northumbria periodically expanded their respective authorities at the expense of the other. Such changeable dominance over smaller territories is glimpsed through the fortunes of Lindsey to the west, first recorded as a semi-independent 'kingdom' under Northumbrian overlordship, but during the reign of Wulfhere being noted as subordinate to Mercia. As Higham puts it, 'there was a very real fluidity to the political boundaries between the Northumbrians and Mercians up to the last two decades of the seventh century' (Higham, 2006, p.398), and even after then such fluidity probably continued for some time afterwards. The ebb and flow of political jurisdiction between these two kingdoms was probably at the expense of all the groups in the north Midlands and southern Yorkshire, and encroachment into the nominal territory of one large kingdom by the other could be gained by the acquisition of one or more of the buffer zones, whilst the nominal 'loser' need not appear to have suffered a serious loss of territorial integrity. The acknowledgement of superior military prowess could thus be shown by the relinquishment of tribute from such territories. Consequently, any notion that the lands of the *Elmedaetna*, *Haethfelthlund*, *Lindes Farona* and the *Pecsaetna* were at all times simply a component part of either Mercia or Northumbria should be entirely dismissed.

South Yorkshire is close to the boundaries of several tribal units. To the south-west was the unit of the *Pecsaetna* in the present-day Derbyshire Peak District. To the south and south-east was an arm of 'original' Mercia (Hart 1977), but its northern boundary at the time of the *Tribal Hidage*'s compilation is unclear. Although there are several natural boundary features such as rivers and ridges, there is no particular topographical or geological change that presented an obvious demarcation to its northern extent. To the west, the limestone Peak District offered a distinct ecozone for the territorial activities of the *Pecsaetna* (Sidebottom, 2020), and to the east, the Magnesian Limestone ridge or the lowlands of the Trent, Ryton and Idle rivers formed natural demarcations in the landscape for the eastern extent of northern Mercia. It was probably the lowland valleys and almost impenetrable marshy landscape of the rivers Idle and Ryton (and in the north, the River Don) that led the people of *Haethfelthlund* to be incorporated with Lindsey to the east when the larger kingdoms were formed. The '*saetna*' names, we think, are Mercian, because the *Tribal Hidage* informs us that there are several groups of people, all with this suffix in certain locations. For example, there are the *Pecsaetna*, the *Magonsaetna* or the *Wreocansaetna*, and within the broad 'umbrella' of the West Saxon entry in the *Tribal Hidage*, the *Wiltsaetna*, *Chilternsaetna* and the *Dorsaetna*. Each of these groups appear to form part of a western arc around the Mercian heartlands (Higham, 1993b, p.85), and it appears that this might be land gained by Mercian expansion over native groups. So it is reasonable to see these as marginal groups in the sense that they are peripheral Mercian satellites which may have had control imposed on them, perhaps by small bands of warrior elite enforcing Mercian control. The same comments could apply to the *Elmedsaetna* in southern Yorkshire.

All of the groups mentioned in the *Tribal Hidage* are allocated a value expressed in hides, with the smallest groups, such as the *Gifla*, allocated 300 hides and the largest – the West Saxons – 100,000 hides. Broadly speaking, a hide is interpreted as the amount of land or economic wealth to support one extended family. The *Pecsaetna* were valued at 1,200 hides (see Fig. 12) and 'original' Mercia at 30,000 hides. By the time that the *Hidage* was compiled, *Haethfelthlund* had already been included with Lindsey and was allocated 7,000 hides. That *Haethfelthlund* was mentioned by name suggests that its incorporation was a recent event, possibly for the purpose of the valuation. The *Elmedsaetna* were allocated 600 hides, half that of the *Pecsaetna* and comparable to small and relatively obscure units such as the *Spalda, Widerigga* or *Bilmigga* and the Isle of Ely, now in Cambridgeshire (Hart, 1977). This raises the question as to whether the allocation of 600 hides to Elmet referred to the whole of what we understand to be a kingdom that might have been roughly coterminous with most of the West Riding of Yorkshire, as it was following the Viking period, or just to a part of it. One avenue of research that may be able to shed some (albeit a little) light on this is that of place-name study (see below).

Loidis, Elmet and Craven

Loidis

In the mid-eighth century, *Loidis* is mentioned by Bede (Sherley-Price, 1955, pp.132, 184) seemingly as a district, although the references are vague and tell us nothing about its status, location or size. It was probably a large 'multiple' estate, essentially one of the building blocks which formed the smaller polities and, in turn, the larger kingdoms. Whether *Loidis* was an integral part of Elmet – one of its large estates – or a small unit with some form of independence at one time is unknown. Jones (1975, p.16) tends to view Elmet and *Loidis* as practically one and the same; Higham suggests it was separate but part of Ceretic's kingdom along with Elmet, and notes that it seems to have been regarded as such by the Northumbrians (Higham, 1993a, p.87). Place-name evidence suggests that *Loidis* was around the Leeds area and that the district included Ledsham and Ledston. These were all to the immediate north of the River Aire, which tends to suggest that *Loidis* was indeed coterminous with Elmet as it was included in the *Tribal Hidage*, or perhaps a large component part of it (Wood, 1996, p.1).

Craven

Craven is another polity of indeterminate status, not known to us until the *Domesday* survey of 1086 when it appears as the district '*Craveseire*' (Wood, 1996, p.1). By then, it seems to have been one of the Yorkshire 'shires', such as Hallamshire, Richmondshire or Allertonshire, which may possibly have been semi-independent units, large multiple estates or (more likely) amalgamations of several estates. The location of the original land unit of Craven is vague, but it seems to have been to the north-west of Elmet (Faull and Moorhouse, 1981, p.171) and was probably one of the smaller units of the North, the parameters of which were possibly determined by its geology and soils and, thereby, its economic cohesion, in pretty much the same way that the *Pecsaetna* of the north Midlands are focused on the Carboniferous Limestone of the southern Pennines (Sidebottom, 2020). Geologically, Craven is crossed by the 'Craven Faults', an area of comparative lowland separated from higher ground to the north. In this latter area are large areas of limestone pavement and limestone scars, the most striking piece of exposed bedrock undoubtedly being Malham Cove (Wood, 1996, p.3).

It seems probable that Craven was once a 'kingdom' – perhaps in the same way that *Loidis* was once regarded – and possibly covered a wide area from the Ribble to Dentdale, perhaps even stretching as far as the southern end of the Lake District, according to Higham (1993a, p.84). Later, it was fossilised in the large wapentake (a subdivision of certain shires, corresponding to a hundred) of Staincliffe, but subsequently subdivided (Wood, 1996, p.1). Like *Loidis*, Craven is a British name and its location placed it firmly in the so-called 'British West' of England. Its relationship with Elmet is unknown, but it may well have been one of the smaller neighbouring kingdoms that Ceretic of Elmet held authority over. Faull and Moorhouse (1981, p.171) suggest that Craven may have fallen to Anglo-Saxon control before Elmet did, providing a route through to the coveted Cheshire Plain.

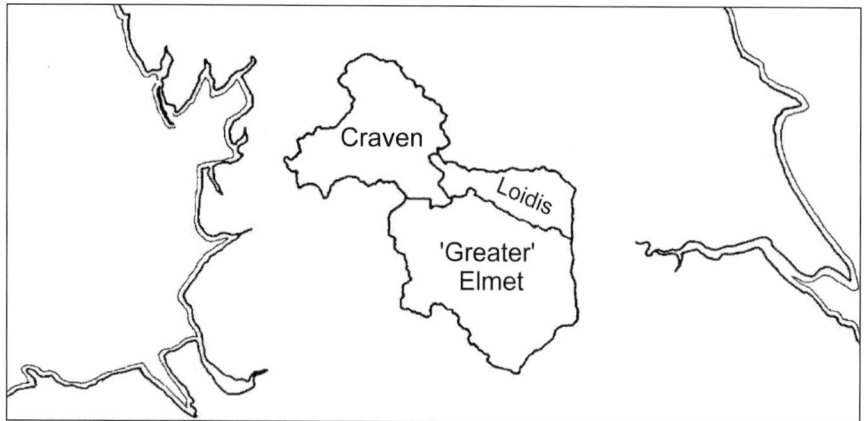

Fig. 14: The location of Elmet, Loidis and Craven (based on Wood, 1996, and Jones, 1975).

Elmet

There is the general assumption that South Yorkshire, as it is today, was the southern part of the kingdom of Elmet, the land unit of the *Elmedsaetna* (see, for example, Faull and Moorhouse, 1981, p.171). This was largely brought about by the later *thriding* boundary that existed after the formation of the West Riding following the Anglo-Scandinavian settlement based on York, and the frontier with those in control of the Scandinavian north-east Midlands. It is only at this point that we have any hint of the territorial arrangements of this part of the region, however vague it may have been. Hart's analysis of the *Tribal Hidage* (1970 and 1977) echoes this vagueness but suggests that the southern reaches of Elmet stretched as far as the *Pecsaetna* and *Haethtfealthlund*, thus, by implication, abutting the north-eastern frontier of Mercia, although where this line of demarcation was then located is unclear. Loveluck concurs that the Elmetian territory stretched eastwards to the Humberhead Levels but southwards only to the River Don (Loveluck, 2003, p.157). Breeze (2002) notes the variation that previous writers have placed on the importance and territorial limits of Elmet, ranging from the view that it was an inconsequential land unit to one that saw it as crucial to the struggles of Gwynedd, Mercia and Northumbria, especially in the early-seventh century. Territorially, Breeze agrees with several writers that there was perhaps an Elmetian heartland between the rivers Aire and Wharfe, but states that the battles fought by Northumbria after the annexation of Elmet took place in the region of the River Idle, south of Doncaster. This suggests that either Elmetian territory extended this far (Breeze, 2002, pp.162–65) or that the southern part of Yorkshire was under direct Northumbrian control, with Elmet sidelined in an insular position largely between the rivers Wharfe and Aire. Given the potential and periodically actual conflict between Mercia and Northumbria, to allow the southern borderlands of Northumbrian power to rest in Elmetian hands seems somewhat implausible, as the latter could, at any time, play kingmaker between the two and had been adversarial towards Northumbria in the past. However, the evidence is that the Anglo-Saxons kept control over Ermine Street, thereby securing an unimpeded route to the east of the *Elmedsaetna*.

But how fixed in the landscape were the boundary parameters of Elmet and, for that matter, Northumbria? It is perhaps not reasonable to regard Elmet as the only polity that existed in the southern Pennine region of Yorkshire. We know from the *Tribal Hidage* that there were numerous small units of the Midlands that comprised the kingdom of Mercia; some of these are only known to us from this document, without which we would never have known of their existence. It is also quite likely that Elmet was a 'broad-brush' term which incorporated several small units under Elmetian control, as Higham suggests (1993a, p.85), which may not have included a part of South Yorkshire. This avenue is explored further below through the evidence from the region.

It is largely the later shire boundary that has led to the notion that Elmet extended to the Yorkshire/Derbyshire boundary, as well as there being no mention of any other tribal unit in southern Yorkshire. However, Derbyshire is not known to us before the eleventh century, and Yorkshire, as it became known, is a product of the Viking control based on York in the later Saxon period. So there is considerable doubt that the old southern shire boundary of Yorkshire is an ancient one, it being more likely that it was created to consolidate a reorganization of Anglo-Scandinavian territorial jurisdiction, as discussed below. The allocation of 600 hides in the *Tribal Hidage* suggests that Elmet was much smaller than the later *thriding*, and Jones points out that just the later wapentakes of Barkston Ash and Skyrack together would have been valued at nearly 600 hides, based on their *Domesday* carucate[1] assessment (Jones, 1975, p.13). These two wapentakes were sandwiched between the rivers Aire and Wharfe, roughly stretching from present-day Selby in the east to Keighley in the west. This is not to say that these wapentakes were, in fact, the original Elmet; they were not likely to have existed then, although they may have been formed from older multiple estates which did form part, at least, of the kingdom of Elmet.

It may well be that Elmet once stretched all the way from the River Wharfe to the River Don. Taking into account the *Tribal Hidage* assessment, this would make sense, although Henson suggests that the reduced hidage assessment might have been a special 'reduced rate' for a newly acquired province to secure loyalty, or a remission of tribute due to war damage (Henson, 2020, p.4), implying that Elmet was geographically bigger than this. Another possibility is that part of this land, between the Don and the Wharfe, contained areas of little economic importance or was largely depopulated and thus did not result in a larger hidage count. Higham (1993a) shows the extent of place-name evidence in southern Yorkshire that suggests woodland cover (Fig. 6). There are several bands of woodland which may have separated small groups in southern Yorkshire, notably large tracts surrounding the postulated heartland of Elmet around *Loidis*; indeed, the 'forest of Elmet' was Bede's description of the area. The Coal Measures sandstones to the south of the River Don, mostly in present-day north-east Derbyshire, may have been another (or part

---

1 A carucate was a unit of land that could be ploughed in a single year by a team of oxen.

of the same) area of extensive woodlands developed as the result of regeneration after the collapse of the Roman economy (see Rackham, 1986, pp.75–83). It has already been mentioned that numerous place-name elements found in the Coal Measures region refer to woodland, and this part of the borderland with northern Mercia may also have been sparsely inhabited during much of the Anglo-Saxon period.

Chapter 4

The Importance of Doncaster

The importance of Doncaster during the Roman period has already been outlined, the Roman military fortification of *Danum* being on the south bank of the navigable reaches of the River Don on a major military road. To the east, the landscape was impassable, and the principal Roman road, Ermine Street, was channelled here to the east of the high ground of the southern Pennines. For the Romans, Ermine Street was one of the most important routes into the northern territories from Britannia Superior in the south and Midlands. In the post-Roman period, Ermine Street was perhaps equally, if not more, important to the Anglo-Saxons, linking most of the major Anglo-Saxon kingdoms in eastern England and avoiding the British West, which was potentially hostile to them. There is another postulated Roman road which could have linked the fort at Templeborough with Ermine Street at a point north of Doncaster (possibly at Thorpe Audlin). There is doubt, however, that this road ever existed, since one of the key features of the Roman road system in this region was a west–east orientation south of the Brigantian border, with only limited north–south routes. Indeed, no trace of this road has ever been found. If such a road did exist here, then it is unlikely to have remained in use after the withdrawal of the Roman military and would have been blocked by the Roman Rig earthworks somewhere in the vicinity of Greasbrough near modern-day Rotherham.

The location of Doncaster, especially during the seventh century, became more important than ever: at the southern reaches of Northumbria and its Pennine satellites on the one hand, and the northern extent of the kingdom of Mercia on the other. To the east of Doncaster were *Heathfelthlund* and Lindsey, disputed territories between the two powerful rival kingdoms, both with a direct route from Northumbria via Doncaster along the Roman road, now Till Bridge Lane. That the Roman fortifications were likely to have been reused by the Anglo-Saxons, or even British groups with military ambitions, is almost certain. Decisive battles took place either to the north, by the River Went, or to the south, near the River Idle. Doncaster would have provided a refuge where troops could muster as and when necessary and be afforded some protection through the surviving Roman fortifications and the area's strategic location.

The minster church of St George in Doncaster is built on the site of the Roman fort of *Danum* and stands at the heart of the modern town, meaning that excavations have been piecemeal and relatively small-scale. One development after another has continued to destroy evidence from the Roman period, and even more so the fragile archaeology of post-Roman activity. Nevertheless, some evidence has come to light; it seems there was a *vicus* attached to the fort to its south and west (South Yorkshire SMR), and one sherd of late-sixth or early-seventh century Anglo-Saxon pottery has been found with (limited) evidence for a *burh* (town) of similar date (Hey, 2003, p.27; South Yorkshire SMR; Cumberpatch, 2016). The extent of this settlement is unknown, but it does show that there was a post-Roman presence in Doncaster, certainly during the early formation of the large kingdoms. Excavations by St George's Church and at Trenchgate have revealed post-Roman ditches which have been interpreted as part of the Saxon-period *burh*. '*Donacestre*' is mentioned in 764 in a list of 'towns' damaged by fire (Parker, 1987, p.31); however, the definition of 'town' is debateable, bearing in mind that Bede sometimes referred to former Roman fort sites as 'cities'. But the evidence for a *burh* at Doncaster, with a waterfront on the Don, is growing, and during the Anglo Scandinavian period, Doncaster could certainly be called a town, although its status beforehand is problematic.

Various alternatives have been suggested for the status of Doncaster in the post-Roman period. It could be that the fort and attendant infrastructure were abandoned at, or more likely before, the traditional date of *c.* 410 when the military withdrew. Alternatively, post-Roman activity may have continued but within a run-down, ruralized town, or perhaps Doncaster carried on as a populated regional focus until it was revitalized in the Anglo-Scandinavian period (see Buckland, 2021). Buckland outlines the problems associated with any conclusion that can be made from the archaeology, not least because of the subsequent destruction of the local post-Roman landscape through the development of the town, as mentioned earlier. 'Dark earth' deposits found through excavation in Doncaster are intriguing in that they can be interpreted in several ways. They could suggest that there was a post-Roman abandonment and represent a natural accumulation of sediment, but the deposits may equally reflect a concentration and intensification of activity, perhaps as an increasingly threatened rural population sought protection within the walled enclosure (Buckland, 2021, p.33). On balance, Buckland suggests the evidence gathered to date indicates that activity certainly continued through the post-Roman period, albeit in a limited fashion, with Doncaster unlikely to have continued as an urban centre; but it was not abandoned. This certainly concurs with what has been suggested above – that the location of Doncaster was strategic to power struggles during the post-Roman period and certainly found itself in a less than peaceful situation.

This was not an environment to foster a post-Roman proto-urban centre, a location likely to be ravaged by war bands at any time, either from the north or the south. The fortifications at Doncaster 'may still have been controlled by an individual – one hesitates to use the term "warlord" – able to practise at least a local 'monopoly of violence' (Buckland, 2021, p.35). If Doncaster did operate as a strategic location rather than a settlement, as suggested here, then the artefactual evidence for occupation is bound to be severely limited. Given the very few remaining opportunities to excavate post-Roman strata anywhere in the modern town, it is hardly surprising that so little has come to light. Doncaster may well have operated as a 'gatekeeper' location from the late sixth century until the Viking settlement of

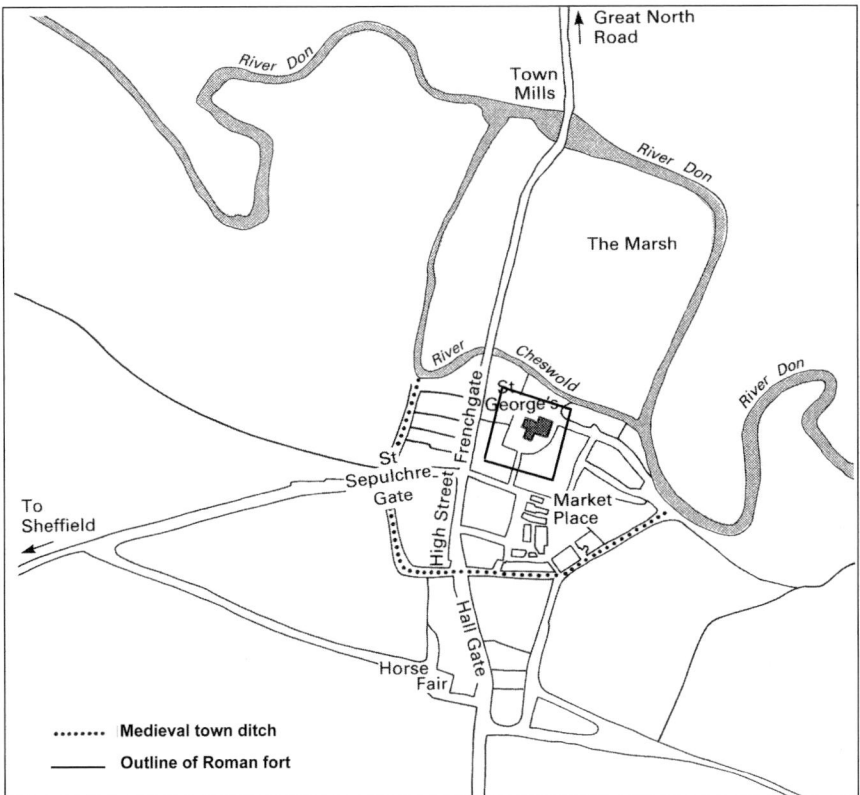

Fig. 15: The site of Doncaster's Roman fort and medieval town (after Hey, 2003, and Buckland, 2021).

the ninth century, when the pottery evidence, especially, suggests a more settled and expanding urban development. Mid-tenth to mid-eleventh-century Torksey and Torksey-type wares are present, and Buckland recorded eight vessels from six sites and another twenty-seven vessels from Church Walk in the town, while 105 sherds (there is no vessel count in the report) were identified as residual elements in later contexts from a site at North Bridge. Individual sherds of various late Saxon-type wares have also been recovered from sites in High Fishergate, High Street and Hallgate, along with evidence for pottery being manufactured in the town (Cumberpatch, 2016). This late Saxon 'revival' of Doncaster, born out of Viking-period developments in the region, will be outlined later in the discussion.

Chapter 5

The Mercian Connection

As discussed above, South Yorkshire seems to have been a frontier between the emerging powers of Northumbria and Mercia, and the border between the two kingdoms appears to have been fluid. There has perhaps always been the assumption that all of Yorkshire was part of Northumbria, although 'Yorkshire' itself is a Viking-Age construct and had no meaning before the later-ninth century at the earliest. The Viking polity based on York and the Anglo-Saxon kingdom of Northumbria were two different entities. We have discussed earlier how natural boundaries, be they topographical or geological, tended to form cohesive land units that operated in a particular economic regime contained within a geological or pedological ecozone. Most of South and West Yorkshire and neighbouring north-east Derbyshire share the same geology (Coal Measures sandstones) and are largely devoid of topographical barriers such as relatively impassable rivers or mountains. As such, there was no specific feature – with the possible exception of the River Don – to enable some form of natural separation between one area and another. This added to the fluidity of control in the region, especially as most of it was in a thinly-populated landscape subject to woodland regeneration after the collapse of the Roman economy.

This section discusses the physical evidence for at least one potential boundary that was created in the South Yorkshire landscape. However, it does appear that Mercian control extended well into southern Yorkshire and existed long enough to leave behind a legacy of place-names and dialects. In 1973, Eduard Kolb published a study on the dialects of the whole of the old West Riding of Yorkshire and how they differ from areas beyond it. Kolb's main objective was to outline the differences between dialectic words in the West Riding and those of the East and North Ridings, and to a lesser extent how certain words pan across the Pennines to the west, beyond the Yorkshire boundary. Kolb's dialect studies also suggested that the Great North Road appears to have been a north–south linguistic boundary, with certain words absent from one side and prevalent on the other. This is, of course, now supported by the archaeological evidence. However, Kolb also saw a significant dialectic region in the Aire–Wharfe area within the West Riding itself, further noting that present-day South Yorkshire and the south-east of West Yorkshire may have shared another similar and localized linguistic origin (Kolb 1973, p.25). Hey also advances evidence from linguistic experts to show that there was a mix of Mercian and Northumbrian words in southern Yorkshire, extending as far northwards as the River Wharfe. He argues that Mercian word forms are the dominant ones in this region, suggesting a significant influx of influence, if not people, from Mercia during the period when Anglo-Saxon linguistics were being formed (Hey, 2003, pp.25–26). Mercian place-name evidence is strongest in the Morley and Agbrigg wapentakes, which were in the south-west of West Yorkshire (Faull and Moorhouse, 1981, p.182), in the same area where Kolb says dialect forms are most distinctive.

'Worth' names are said to be Mercian in origin, and there are eighteen in southern Yorkshire (see Fig. 17), along with Dungworth, Hawksworth and Sugworth, which could have been three unnamed berewicks[2] in Hallamshire (Hey, 2003, pp.27, 31). Aldred suggests that these settlement sites may have been of military or civil defence importance, protecting and providing governance to the boundary regions of an expanding Mercia, or perhaps indicative of the consolidation of Mercian authority in later years (Aldred, 2016, p.1). Apart from the cluster of 'worth' names in, and just north of, South Yorkshire, there is another between the rivers Calder and Wharfe which appears to be describing an area similar to that suggested as

---

2 A berewick is a dependent settlement within a manor.

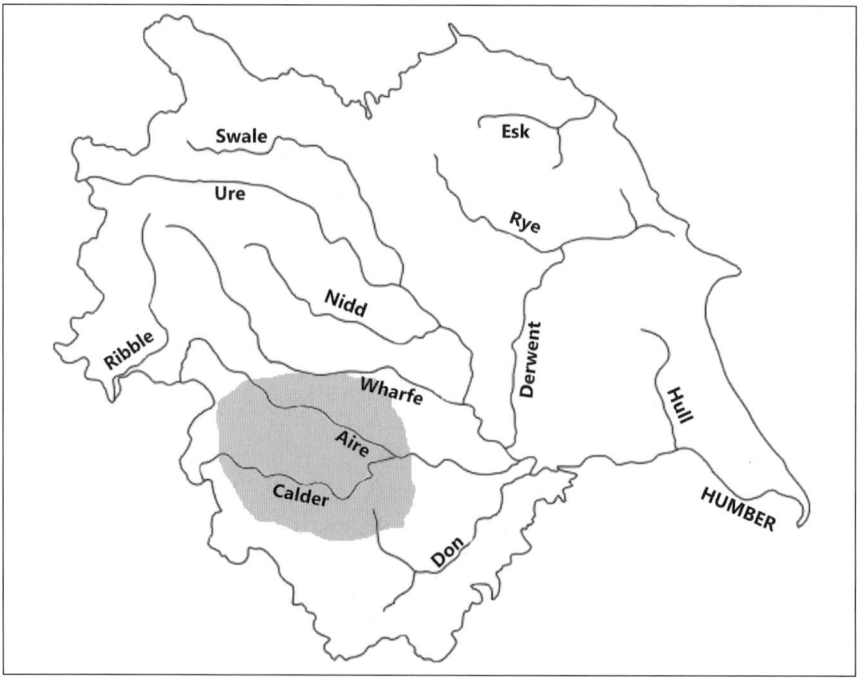

Fig. 16: Kolb's area of concentrated linguistic development.

the heartland of Elmet around *Loidis* (see above). They include such as Hainworth, Haworth, Oakworth, Cullingworth and Hawksworth. These two clusters of 'worth' names suggest that Mercian control extended to include pretty much the old kingdom of Elmet. However, the clusters were not necessarily synchronous in their origins. Whilst one 'worth' name might be the product of early annexation by Mercia, another may well represent a secondary incursion or expansion because many of the 'worth' place-names in South Yorkshire are minor and secondary settlements. For example, Ingbirchworth contains an Old Norse element and the form of the name suggests a Hiberno-Norse input similar to that of the Cumbrian place-name Aspatria, where the first two elements are transposed from the usual format. So it may be that the Mercian name-forms continued to be used for relatively-new settlements, suggesting that a deal of Mercian linguistics were entrenched in the region.

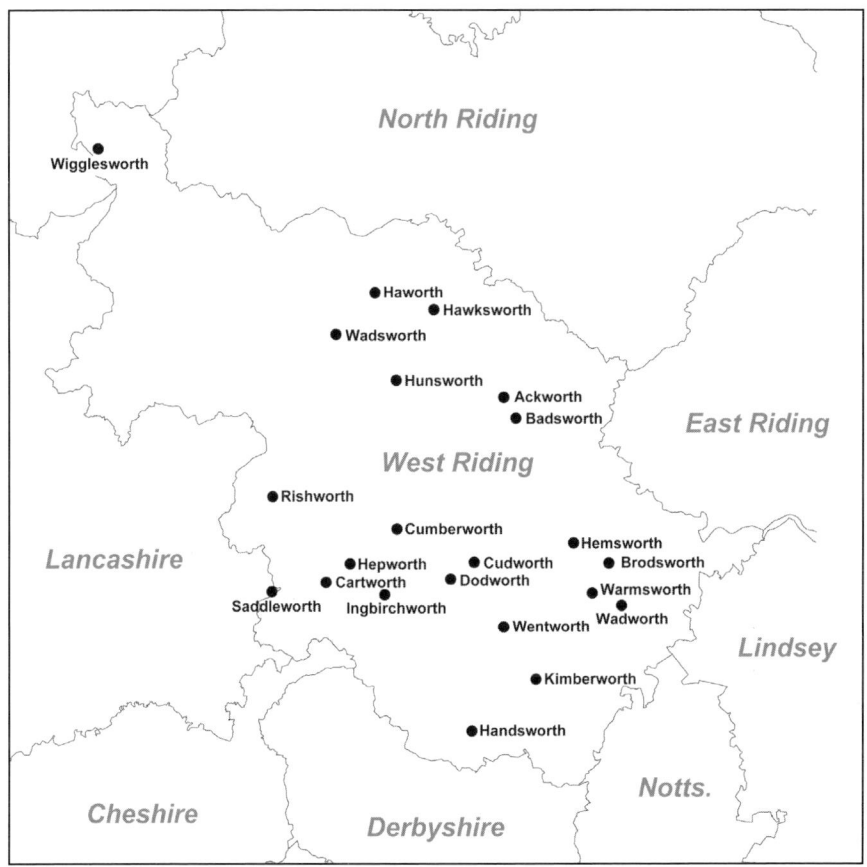

Fig. 17: 'Worth' place-names in south-western Yorkshire.

A number of place-names include the element 'Wala', which is taken to mean names referring to British settlements (as in 'Wales'), although Faull and Moorhouse suggest that some examples may refer to the Mercian *waella* (stream), *wald* (wood) or *wall* (wall). However, the archaeological evidence for an Anglo-Saxon presence is limited in southern Yorkshire, to say the least, and certainly not enough on which to base any conclusions. However, a probably sixth century brooch found at Templeborough Roman fort appears to have been of Mercian origin, suggesting that at least the southernmost reaches of the Don were subject to Mercian pressure from an early date (Jones, 1975, p.24). A gold and niello ring from later in the Anglo-Saxon period was found between Aberford and Sherburn, now in West Yorkshire, inscribed with the name of Aethelswith, queen of Mercia (853–888); but it was found close to the Great North Road and may have been dropped by a traveller (Faull and Moorhouse, 1981, p.187). However, pottery with a Mercian stamp from the fifth or sixth century was recovered from a sunken building in Parlington Hollins near Leeds in West Yorkshire, suggesting that this was more than a casual loss (Roberts, 2018, p.187).

Some might argue that the most compelling evidence for a Mercian presence in southern Yorkshire is the inclusion of the *Elmedsaetna* in the *Tribal Hidage*, as mentioned above. It is usually assumed that this extension (if that is what it was) of Mercian control was relatively short-lived and refers to a period when Mercia was in the ascendancy, and that it probably quickly reverted to the Northumbrian control that was evident when Ceretic was subordinate to its king Edwin. But the linguistics argue otherwise, suggesting that Mercian dominance in the region was much greater and lasting, which is supported by the archaeological evidence, limited though it may be (see also Roberts, 2018, p.191). The Mercia/Northumbria border has always been ambiguous (Kolb, 1973, p.312), but it does seem that at one time or another, South Yorkshire occupied the front line between the two kingdoms and that Mercia had more than a passing interest in the county.

Chapter 6

The Northumbrian Frontier

So far we have discussed the role of the old Roman fortified site at Doncaster and its likely role in the tensions between the emerging kingdoms, especially during the late-sixth and seventh centuries. Doncaster formed a gateway between Mercia and Northumbria, to reinforce this contiguous earthworks above the northern bank of the River Don were either constructed or reused, or possibly additional defences were added to earlier Iron-Age defences across the southern Brigantian border. The dating of these and other earthworks in the region (see below) is problematic and in many cases they remain undated, although some can be attributed to the post-Roman period. The distribution of all these earthwork features tells of a fluid frontier which periodically stretched from well into present-day West Yorkshire to the Don Valley in South Yorkshire. Those earthwork defences in South Yorkshire can also be coupled with place-name evidence, as discussed below.

The earthworks

South Yorkshire and its surrounding region contain a number of earthworks, suggesting that the area has been regarded as a frontier, perhaps for some considerable time. They take the form of relatively short sections of banks and ditches that appear to have protected or demarcated communication routes in and out of specific land units, and are often referred to as 'cross-dykes'. The earthworks are better seen in the regional context, rather than those simply contained within South Yorkshire's modern boundary. Fig. 18 shows the location of

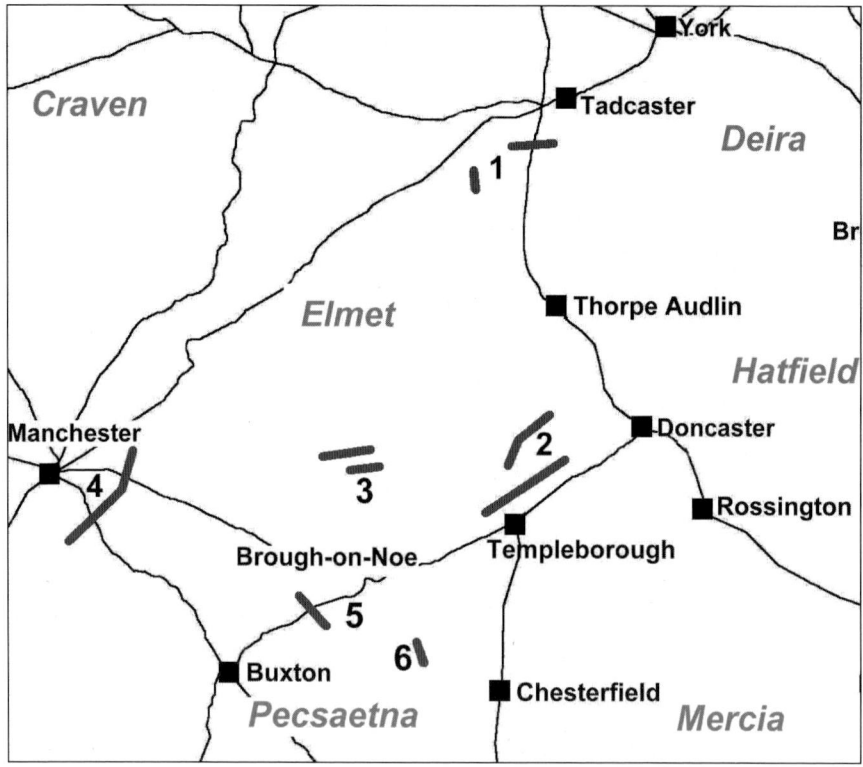

Fig. 18: 'Dyke' earthworks in the region.

these earthworks, including those outside of South Yorkshire, for example, close to Manchester, in the northern Peak District and at Aberford in West Yorkshire. The problem is that only a small number of these are securely dated, and where dates are available, they show a range of periods for when they were constructed – from the Iron Age right through to the post-Roman period. Grigg makes an interesting point that early-medieval 'dyke' earthworks in central England are almost all on the periphery of the kingdom of Mercia, with none in its interior, suggesting that they were erected because of the alarm caused by the rapid rise in the power of this emerging kingdom (Grigg, 2018, p.82).

The Aberford Dykes (Fig. 19) are a series of banks and ditches to either side of the Roman road from Doncaster to Castleford and

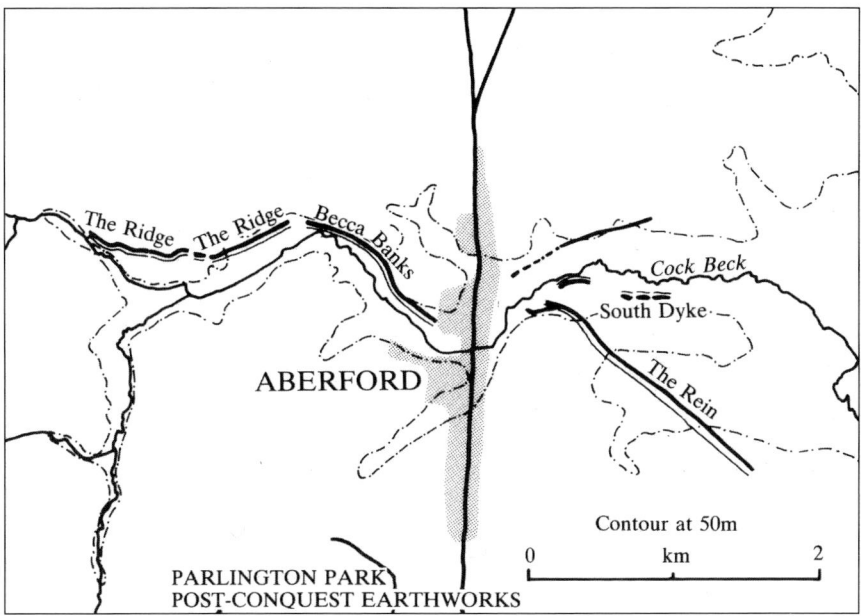

Fig. 19: The Aberford earthworks (from Higham, 1993a).

beyond, utilizing Cock Beck as a line of demarcation and thus adding
to a natural defensive barrier. Some of the banks and ditches appear
to defend from the north, others from the south and east (Higham,
1993a, p.87). The arrangement suggests that they were constructed
after the Roman occupation, and indeed Higham sees them as having
defended the small unit of *Loidis* from Elmet or possibly (and more
likely) being to defend Elmet itself against incursions from the east.
Another short linear earthwork just to the east of Leeds – Grim's
Ditch – is thought to have also demarked the boundary of *Loidis*
(Historic England Listing No. 1020350), but again could have been a
one-time boundary to 'greater Elmet'. Part of the earthwork complex
at Aberford – the 'Becca Banks' and 'The Rig' – were thought to
have been constructed by Northumbrian kings against Mercian
attack (Higham, 1993a, p.87; Jones, 1975, p.25). However, recent
radiocarbon dating shows a range of dates, putting some of the
earthworks in the early Iron Age, possibly before 400 BC, with other
earthwork sections placed at the end of the Roman period. Together

with evidence for ditch re-cutting, this suggests they were first cut during the earlier Iron Age, with redefinition in the late Iron Age or late-Roman period (Chadwick, 2019, p.28). Excavations at the nearby Grim's Ditch also suggest that this was an Iron-Age earthwork that remained in use through the Roman period (Historic England Listing No. 1020350).

The radiocarbon dates show that the Aberford Dykes – or at least some of the earthworks there – existed over a long period of time. That the Roman road passed through the complex suggests that it protected or demarked a boundary along a pre-existing routeway to the north which was incorporated into the Roman military infrastructure. Aberford lies on the Magnesian Limestone ridge which also runs through South Yorkshire, and it is possible that, like Ryknield Street in South Yorkshire, a long-distance Iron Age route became 'Romanized'. This would also have the effect of taking communication routes out of the control of the native populace. As a boundary, which could also form a defensive measure, it is quite possible – if not probable – that the earthworks remained in use through the post-Roman period, and its suggested use as a later defence against Anglo-Saxon incursions is highly plausible.

The Nico Ditch, to the east of Manchester, is a linear ditch and bank, with its ditch on the south-eastern side, extending over some considerable distance, appearing to protect three Roman roads as they begin to converge on Manchester. Its date is unknown but its relationship with the Roman roads and proximity to the early-medieval *burh* and the old Roman fort at Manchester strongly suggest a late-Roman or Anglo-Saxon provision. It is also suggested that it may have formed part of the boundary of the kingdom of Rheged in the sixth century, or have been the limit of the kingdom of Mercia in the eighth century (Historic England Listing No. 1016197), as generally suggested by Grigg (2018, p.82). Whatever the date of the Nico Ditch, Higham likens it to a mirror version of the defensive earthworks on the north bank of the River Don which are described below (Higham, 1993a, p.143), and again it seems to be just one of the linear demarcatory features in the region between Mercia and Northumbria (see Fig. 18).

In the northern limestone Peak District are two earthworks which seem to protect the Peak from the north-east: the Grey Ditch and the Calver Cross Dyke. The Grey Ditch is a bank and ditch which appears to form a checkpoint across the Roman road travelling southwards from the Roman fort at Brough-on-Noe (Navio) into the White Peak of present-day northern Derbyshire (see Fig. 20). Through excavation we know that it is post-Roman in date (Guilbert and Taylor, 1992). Although the Grey Ditch has previously been seen as a defensive or demarcatory measure made by Mercia against Northumbrian attack (see Hart, 1977, p.53), it lies much further to the south than all other earthworks suggested to have served this function. The writer has made the case that its construction was to form a line of demarcation to separate and defend the land unit of the *Pecsaetna* (the 'Peak Dwellers') and their primary interest in the production of lead. It stands almost exactly on the north-eastern limit of the limestone where lead ore is found (Sidebottom, 2020, p.26). A few miles to the south-east stands the Calver Cross Dyke, a short length of double bank-and-ditch to the east of Bakewell. It is undated and has been severely damaged by limestone quarrying over the centuries. There are similarities between this earthwork and the Grey Ditch. Again, the Calver Cross Dyke lies on the north-eastern limit of the limestone and appears to stand across an ancient routeway. As far as we know, this was not a Roman road, but it may well have been a principal routeway in use during the Saxon period. It is tempting to see the Calver Cross Dyke as another Anglo-Saxon period construction to define the territorial extent of the *Pecsaetna*.

In South Yorkshire, there are two sets of earthworks. One of these is known as the Bar Dyke, which lies at the edge of moorland, 3km north-west of Bradfield. It presently stands across two routeways and forms a line of demarcation across a break in a Millstone Grit escarpment. One of the routes heads south-east towards Bradfield and the confluence of the rivers Don and Loxley, while the other is shown

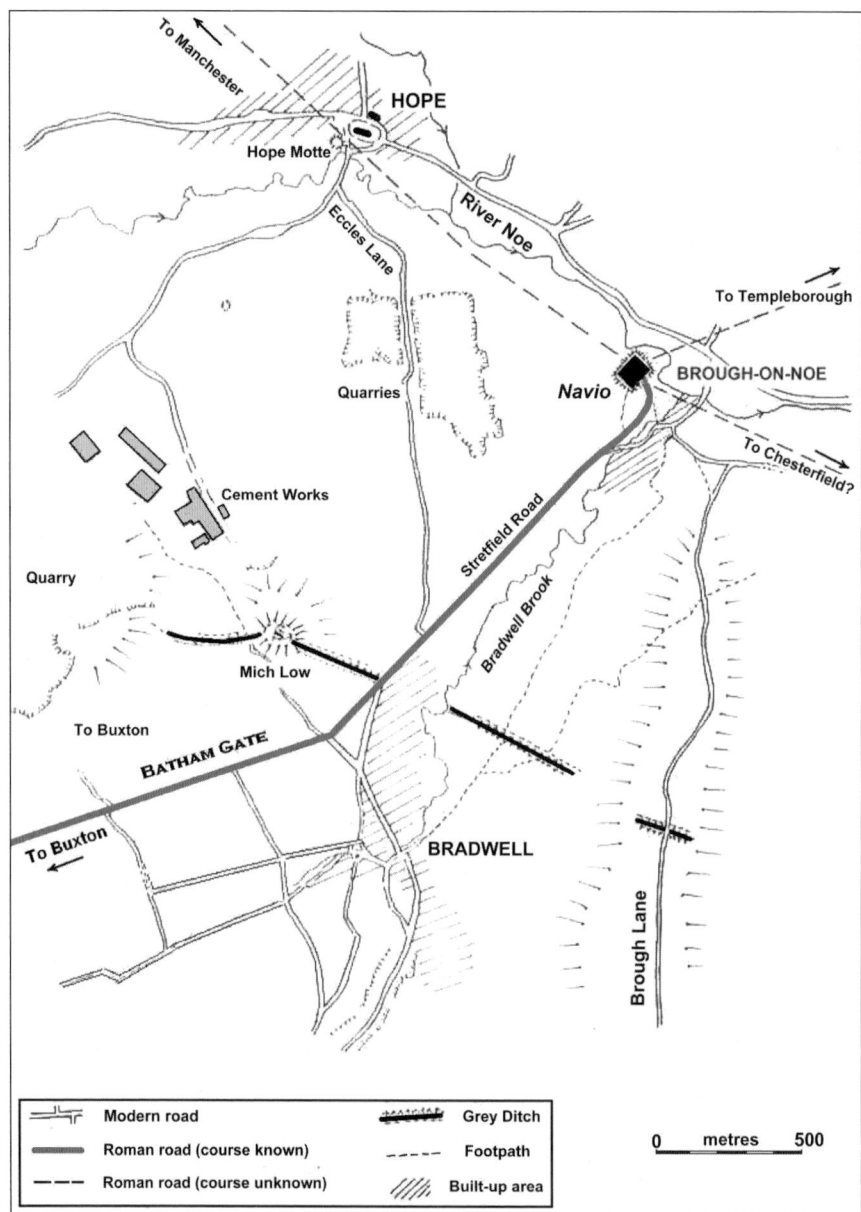

Fig. 20: The Grey Ditch.

as a 'bridleway' by Jefferys (1771), travelling south-west towards the River Derwent, now in Derbyshire; to the north is Penistone in the upper Don Valley. The antiquity of these routeways is unknown, but presumably at least one of them was a significant thoroughfare when the earthwork was constructed. The Bar Dyke earthwork, which is still in reasonably good condition, has its ditch to the north, suggesting that it was intended to defend land to the south of it.

The Bar Dyke is undated but is thought to be either Iron Age or post-Roman (Historic England 2020, Listing No. 1017508). Both Bradfield and Penistone have pre-Conquest associations; Penistone has an Anglo-Saxon period stone monument built into the nave of the church, while Bradfield also has a pre-Conquest stone monument and was the location of an early Norman motte-and-bailey castle which would have overlooked the routeway from the north passing through the Bar Dyke. Again, this is an earthwork which could have originally been constructed in the prehistoric era but reused when tribalism re-emerged after the collapse of Roman administration. If the Bar Dyke is seen in an Iron Age or Roman context, then this would suggest that it stood at a point where the Corieltauvi were creating a demarcation or defence against the Brigantians, or it was possibly part of the Roman offensive against the latter. In a post-Roman context, the earthwork might suggest an offensive by Mercia to claim territory from the Northumbrians or to prevent Northumbrian expansion to the south. About 2 km to the north-west of the Bar Dyke is the Broomhead Dyke, which is also a bank-and-ditch with the ditch on the north side. It bisects a prehistoric cairn field, suggesting that it dates to a later period. The earthwork has been damaged by drainage works but has clearly been used as a local boundary, the latter continuing on the opposite side of the road that links it to the Bar Dyke, and thus both earthworks straddle the same routeway. It is tempting to see the Broomhead Dyke and Bar Dyke as a reflection of the double lines of defences of the Roman Rig, described below, but this is of course conjectural.

Overlooking the Don Valley, between the Iron Age hillfort at Wincobank (now in Sheffield) and the River Dearne in South Yorkshire, is a series of bank-and-ditch earthworks known as the Roman Rig (or Roman Ridge). They comprise two lines of earthworks

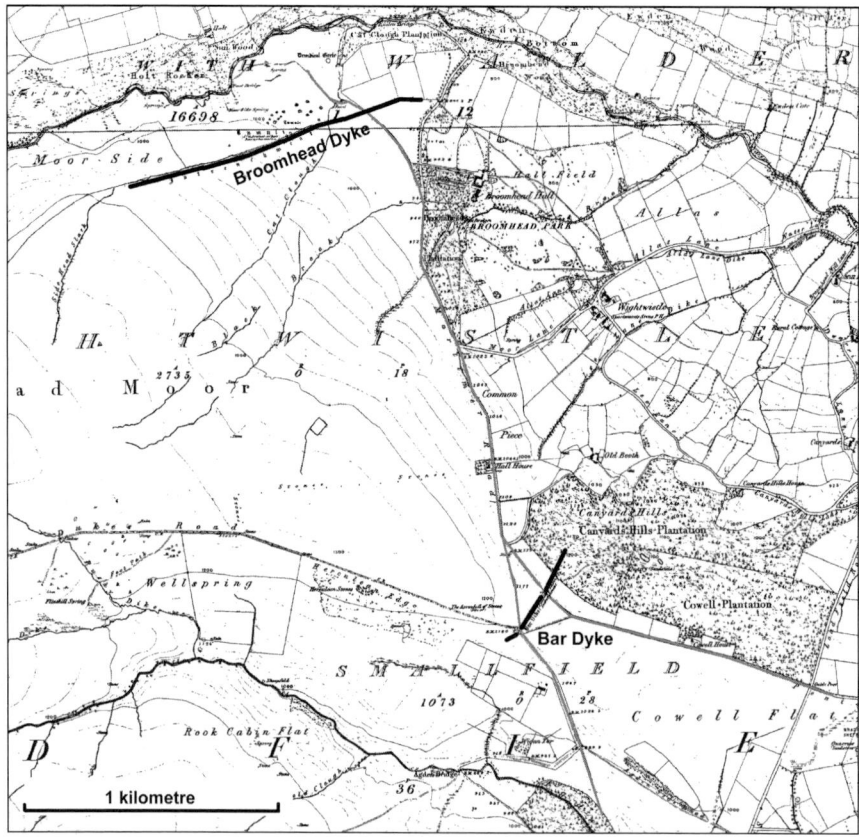

Fig. 21: The Bar Dyke and Broomhead Dyke in 1855 (based on Ordnance Survey 1855).

aligned south-west–north-east and survive for 27km, extending to the north-east towards Mexborough, where they cease to be traceable any further (Chadwick, 2019, p.28). The earthworks remain undated and it is not known whether the two lines are contemporary. There is evidence that the ditches were re-cut, suggesting that 'the earthworks have much more complex histories than is visible from the surface' (ibid.). There have been several interpretations of their function and date. Boldrini (1999, p.103) suggested an Iron-Age date for the Rig, demarking territory between the Brigantes and Corieltauvi, but concluded that the earthworks could have been renewed in later periods, as suggested for those elsewhere.

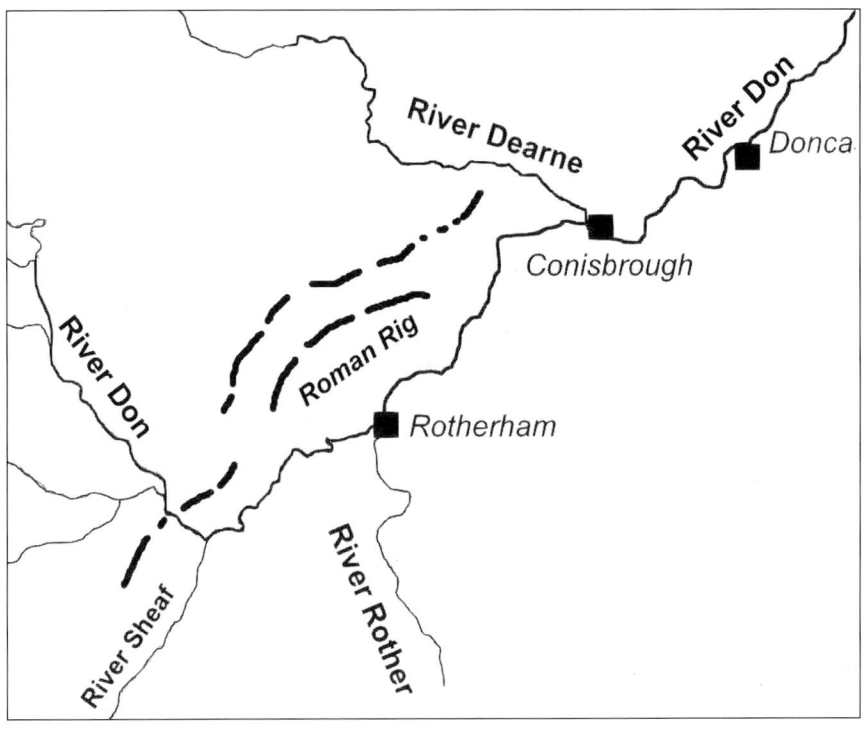

Fig. 22: Roman Rig Earthworks.

Fig. 23. Roman Rig
earthworks at Abdy,
near Wath-upon-Dearne.
(Photo by E. Palmer)

Despite a possibly earlier date for the original construction of the Roman Rig earthworks, they may have been re-manned in the post-Roman period (see Higham, 2006, p.406). Adding to this hypothesis, the Roman Rig earthworks can be seen in the context of the unusual concentration of '*burh*' place-names in the same area, of which eight still survive (see below), and suggests that both the '*burh*' names and the Roman Rig were focussed on the strategically-important post-Roman routeway through Doncaster (Higham, 1993a, pp.142–43). Hey (2003, pp.23–24) also considers that the Roman Rig could have been used in post-Roman context as a territorial defence in the struggles between Northumbria and Mercia, perhaps demarking the southern boundary of Elmet. However, that there are two lines of earthworks tends to argue that they were intended as more than a line of demarcation. The northern range of the Roman Rig was used to demark parish boundaries (ibid.), suggesting that when the parishes were formed they were still pertinent landscape features. It is perhaps worth mentioning that a linear earthwork of a bank and ditch was discovered at Conisbrough Parks on the south bank of the River Don to the south of Denaby. It was overlain by ridge-and-furrow, so could possibly be early medieval (Stein, 2019, p.12). If this is the case, then the earthwork may have been related to the protection of the northern end of Ryknield Street close to the crossing at Strafford Sands.

'Burgh' place-name evidence

There are a number of place-names in South Yorkshire that, together, suggest a fortified frontier, and many have seen this as evidence of the Northumbrian or Elmetian frontier. The main problem is that we have little idea when these place-names first came into existence. Fig. 24 shows the distribution of these names, all of which contain the element 'burgh', an Anglo-Saxon term taken to mean a fortified place. Hey points out that there are two clusters of these names in

South Yorkshire, one forming a string of place-names following the line of the Roman Rig earthworks, especially to the east of it and culminating near Doncaster (Hey, 2003, p.28). The second cluster is to the north-west of the earthworks and is located around the upper reaches of the River Dearne.

Those place-names that relate to the Roman Rig earthworks (east to west) are Sprotbrough, Conisbrough, Barnburgh, Mexborough and Greasbrough. Apart from Greasbrough, which is located within the surviving line of the earthworks near present-day Rotherham, they are all clustered around the crossing of the Don at Strafford Sands (Hey, 2003, p.28), via the 'Romanized' Ryknield Way, a route which seems to have linked with Ermine Street to the north and thus could have provided an alternative for a military force from the south (or the north, for that matter) to avoid Doncaster. These defensive locations were in a position to provide military support against invaders, or at least act as border checkpoints. Of these fortified locations, we are pretty sure that Conisbrough was an early centre which gained in importance, especially after the Scandinavian settlement of the area (see below). Along with Conisbrough, both Mexborough and Barnburgh have Anglo-Saxon period stone monuments, which suggests they were estate centres by the tenth century, as discussed below. At Sprotbrough, pottery finds of eleven sherds of Anglo-Saxon wares represented ten vessels dating to between the late-ninth and early-mid-eleventh century (Cumberpatch, 2016). All of these place-names, including Greasbrough, are included in the *Domesday* survey of 1086 (Williams and Martin, 1992, pp.828–29). It is possible that Greasbrough may have been on a Roman road from Templeborough to Thorpe Audlin (see Ordnance Survey 2011), as mentioned earlier, but no trace of it has yet been found. Several more-recent studies have disregarded this route entirely (see for example Ottaway, 2003, p.126). Not far from Greasbrough is Aldwarke ('old work'), which may refer to a section of the Roman Rig earthworks no longer extant. The strategic location of the area is supported by the Norman need to erect fortifications at both

Conisbrough and Mexborough (Hey, 2003, pp.68–69), but in what way these locations were fortified – if at all – during the Anglo-Saxon period is unknown.

The second set of 'burgh' place-names – Kexbrough, Stainborough, Worsbrough and Measbrough (Dike) – cluster around the higher reaches of the River Dearne near present-day Barnsley (see Fig. 24); all of them, except Measbrough Dike (now a district of Barnsley), appear in the *Domesday* survey (Williams and Martin, 1992, p.825). Whilst a relationship between the Greasbrough–Sprotbrough cluster of 'burgh' names and the defensive earthworks of the Roman Rig seems tenable, those in the upper Dearne Valley do not show any relationship with known defensive structures.

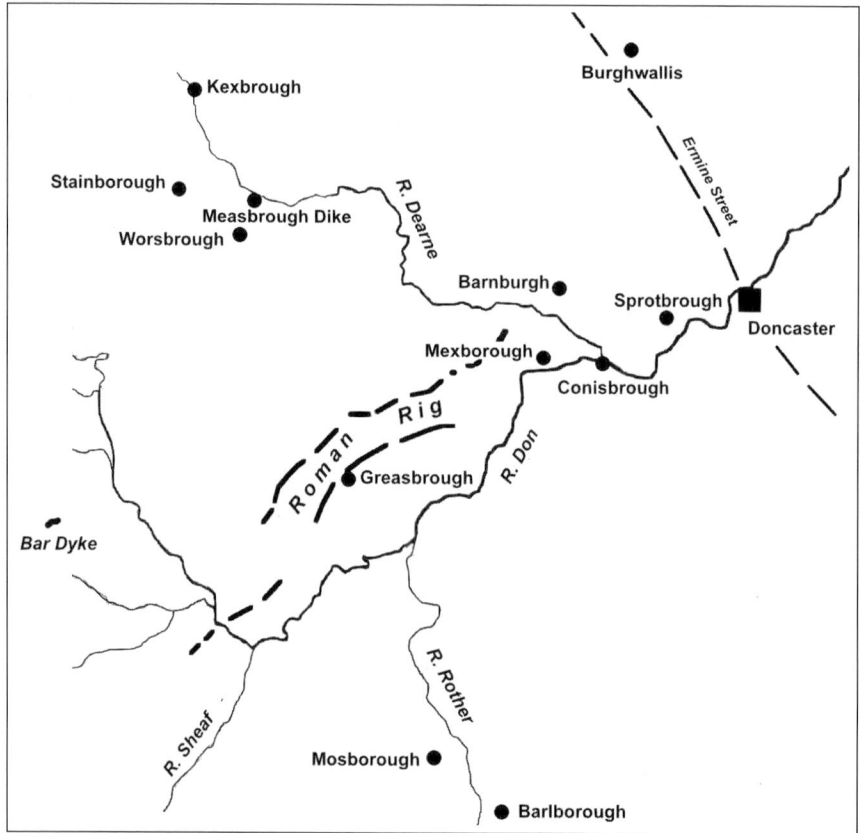

Fig. 24: 'Burgh' place-names.

A Norman motte-and-bailey castle was built at Stainborough, which suggests it once occupied a strategic location, but no other evidence presents itself to explain this cluster of place-names. Hey (2003, p.28) suggests the possibility that they may have been Mercian strongholds during a period of their advancement as far as the River Dearne, but this is entirely conjectural, although the existence of an ancient routeway into this area which passed through the Bar Dyke is quite possible.

There are two other 'burgh' place-names in the south of the region which may be simply fortuitous and never had a 'fortified site' status – Mosborough and Barlborough, which lay just either side of the present Derbyshire–Yorkshire border. Both are included in the *Domesday* survey. Barlborough was included with Whitwell, and both were the subject of charters by Wulfric Spott, suggesting that they were relatively new estate holdings at the beginning of the eleventh century and unlikely to have had any great antiquity (see discussion on charters, below). However, that they stood along what became the border between the Danelaw counties of Derbyshire and Yorkshire may have been significant, and the close proximity to Whitwell and also Sherwood Forest to its east meant that both locations may have been regarded as significant border places.

Chapter 7

Vikings and the Later-Saxon Period

As with the Anglo-Saxons beforehand, it is fairly clear that the southern Pennines were not central to the interests of the Viking incomers. Although exerting control over a wide area, the Scandinavians were primarily interested in taking control of the richer agricultural lands of eastern England, such as the Vale of York, Lincolnshire and the Midlands lowlands. Three major polities emerged within the Viking-controlled areas of England: the Vikings of East Anglia, those of the north-east Midlands and – most powerful of all – the Vikings of York. The initial Viking invasion and settlement of Lincolnshire is little understood (Sawyer, 1998, p.96), but it seems that the Lincoln Vikings had close ties with those of York and were probably under their authority at least by 890 (Stafford, 1985, p.114), and this no doubt also applied to *Haethfelthlund*. In the 890s, it is recorded that Alfred the Great negotiated with the York Vikings over land which is now in the south of Lincolnshire (ibid., p.114) which shows, incidentally, that the modern county had not begun to take shape until after the Viking settlement. The Scandinavian control based on York, therefore, was extensive, although the *Anglo-Saxon Chronicles* (Garmonsway, 1953) includes little information on the power relationships within the new Anglo-Scandinavian kingdom of York, especially with the old kingdom of Elmet.

Disruption in Anglo-Saxon settlement patterns and changes in landholding occurred in England followed the Scandinavian settlement (Stattel, 2020, p.9), but in areas which were not the primary focus for the Scandinavians these changes may have been relatively minimal, especially in the short term. Similar comments are made by Hadley (1996, p.6) when considering the large estates in South

Yorkshire, and she concludes that the large 'multiple' estates were not, necessarily, ancient units but formed well after the initial Viking settlement in the later-Saxon period. This indeed appears to have been pertinent in South Yorkshire, especially to land south of the River Don where political events of the tenth century suggest that major landholding changes are likely to have followed some considerable time later, as discussed below. The extent of the initial Scandinavian settlement in southern Yorkshire is difficult to identify, not least because Anglo-Scandinavian material culture was initially not so different from their Germanic predecessors. Only in a few places in northern England, where there was a concentrated Scandinavian presence with evidence for high-status, manufactured and imported goods, does an 'ethnically Scandinavian' presence show itself clearly in the archaeological record; *Jorvik* (York) is an obvious example. But on a rural day-to-day level, the Scandinavian incomers were more likely to adopt the material culture of their surroundings, so it is difficult to isolate a Scandinavian presence from any other. However, there are other factors that can suggest the extent of Scandinavian control in the region.

As with the Saxon incomers, 'pagan' burial evidence provides an indication of the extent of early Scandinavian incursions, where grave goods and, in recent times, chemical analysis can identify a Scandinavian presence. Only one such burial has been found in South Yorkshire, although those of Scandinavian descent in later Christian burial places will have escaped the archaeological record. Indeed, Hadley (2002) notes that during the Viking period there was a variety of burial practices used in northern England and a range of cemetery sites used (often for short periods), all of which makes identification even more difficult. However, in 2001, the remains of a late-ninth or possibly early tenth-century Viking inhumation burial (probably an adult female) was recovered from a grave cut through a Romano-British ditch at Adwick-le-Street to the north of Doncaster on the Roman road of Ermine Street (Speed and Walton-Rogers, 2004). The reader will recall that earlier in this discussion, Anglo-Saxon burial evidence was also discovered at Adwick, where in 2007 an Anglo-Saxon cemetery was unearthed (McKinley, 2016), and the Viking burial was discovered only a few hundred metres to the north-west of this site. Geophysics in the early 1980s suggested that there were more burials in this area, but no excavation was carried out (Speed and Walton-Rogers, 2004, p.54); however, these were not necessarily Viking-Age. Chemical analysis of the burial remains suggested that the individual most likely came from Norway, although a Scottish origin could not be ruled out (ibid., pp.60–63).

Like the earlier Anglo-Saxon cemetery, the Viking-period interment flanked the eastern side of Ermine Street in an area used for burials from the Roman period onwards. This location suggests that it was associated with early-Scandinavian activity in and around Doncaster and, in similar fashion to their Anglo-Saxon predecessors, indicates that this may have been part of a military or transient movement across the old borderlands between the two kingdoms, now under Scandinavian control. Occasional finds in the immediate region, which could be attributed to a Viking presence, tell a similar story. A Trewhiddle-style[3] strap-terminal, dating from the ninth century, has been found at Skelbrooke, and a gold, garnet and glass brooch of tenth or eleventh-century origin was found near Bawtry, along with an earlier find of a small Viking-style iron axe-head (McKinley, 2016, p.55). Also from Bawtry, a small sherd of probable late-Saxon coarse sandy ware and a putative tenth-century building was also discovered (Cumberpatch, 2016). Skelbrooke is about 2.5km north of Adwick-le-Street, and again on the route of Ermine Street; the finds from the Bawtry area are from about 20km to the south-east, but are also related to the same Roman road as it enters the local area from Lincoln. It seems, therefore, that the early Viking presence in southern Yorkshire was more focussed on the protection

---

3 The Trewhiddle style, generally found on Anglo-Saxon metalwork, takes its name from the Trewhiddle Hoard, which was found in 1774 near Trewhiddle in Cornwall. Intricately carved decoration in this style includes silver with niello inlay, and motifs include animal and plant interlace and geometric patterns.

of borderlands and exerting local control than on obtaining land for settlement.

Place-names provide some evidence that Scandinavian settlement did leave its mark in the South Yorkshire landscape. In very broad and simple terms, there are two forms of place-names that usually denote either primary or secondary Scandinavian settlement. Place-names ending '...by' often indicate primary Scandinavian settlements, while those ending in '...thorpe' indicate secondary settlements. Having said that, 'thorpe' is not exclusively a Scandinavian term, so one must exercise some caution here. The primary settlements – ending in '...by' – are taken to be those formed early in the Scandinavian takeover of central places that were formerly under Anglo-Saxon control. Throughout the Anglo-Saxon and Anglo-Scandinavian periods, the large estates – 'multiple estates' as they are known – were gradually broken up into smaller units, which eventually led to the formation of 'manors' that were documented in late Saxon wills, charters and the *Domesday* survey; this will be discussed further below. This process of estate fragmentation continued through the Anglo-Scandinavian period, and the '...by' place-names often refer to an early-Scandinavian phase of this. The existing estate centre usually retained its Anglo-Saxon name, but that portion that became separated through fragmentation was given a Scandinavian name ending in '...by'. A good example is Conisbrough and Cadeby, where Conisbrough seems to have been the existing estate centre and Cadeby a portion of that estate created as a separate (but probably dependent) landholding during the Anglo-Scandinavian period. In Lincolnshire, Scandinavian '...by' place-names are found pretty much throughout the county alongside names of Anglo-Saxon origin, nicely illustrating the process of fragmentation of the older Saxon estates, with new Scandinavian-period lesser manors appearing in parts of the old and larger estate.

West Yorkshire has only nine '...by' names (Faull and Moorhouse, 1981, p.206), while '...by' place-names occur only in specific parts of South Yorkshire They are found along the navigable portion of the River Don, from Barnby (Dun) in the east to Denaby, near Conisbrough, in the west. There are also three '…by' names which follow the Magnesian Limestone ridge – Firsby, Maltby and Hellaby – the latter producing a single sherd of Lincoln Kiln-type ware dated to between the mid-ninth and early-eleventh century (Cumberpatch, 2016). These Scandinavian names either follow the route of Ryknield Street or, in the case of Maltby, are just off it, on the western fringes of the Magnesian Limestone ridge. The distribution of '…by' names suggests that this was not a normal 'organic' settlement pattern, but more strategic in that it appears to be limited to the control of communications – the River Don and the routeway that crossed it close to the fortified sites on its northern bank. Coupled with the Viking burial evidence at Adwick – limited though it is – this distribution suggests that Viking infiltration in South Yorkshire was similar to that of the earlier Saxon incursions.

The '…thorpe' names, on the other hand, are generally considered to be further along the process of fragmentation, being given both

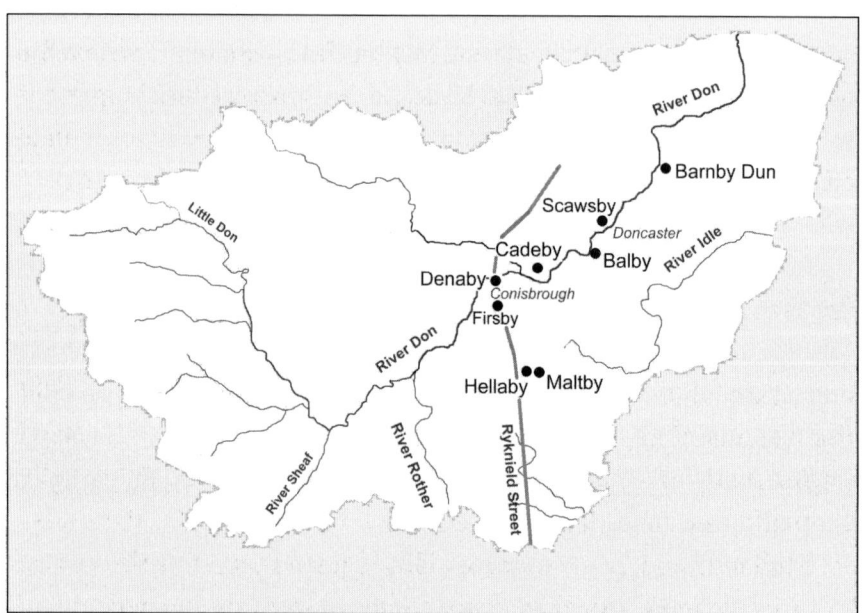

Fig. 25: '…by' place-names in South Yorkshire.

before and after the Norman Conquest (Faull and Moorhouse, 1981, p.205). 'Thorpe', roughly translated, refers to a farmstead or small landholding which was often located on marginal land, in many cases on the periphery of one of the large estates and an area of little previous agricultural exploitation. Some, if not many, of the '...thorpe' place-names were likely to have been formed by Norse immigrants who were adept at farming hillslope landscapes and were able to make the most of the less favourable agricultural land of the estate. One particular Norse group likely to have been involved in such settlement formation – the 'Hiberno-Norse' – is described below.

One feature of the Viking settlement was the formation of urban centres, such as York, Lincoln, Derby or Stamford. In southern Yorkshire, only one urban centre appears to have developed, at Doncaster, where, as discussed earlier, there is archaeological and documentary evidence that it became an urban centre from the Viking settlement of the ninth century until its fortunes diminished during the eleventh century (Parker, 1987, pp.33–37). Doncaster's revival in the late-Saxon period was all part of the Anglo-Scandinavian development of southern Yorkshire. Today, '...gate' street-names – such as Hall Gate, French Gate and Baxter Gate – are found within the medieval core of Doncaster and largely cluster around the footprint of the Roman defences. '*Gat*' (gate) was the Old Norse term for a road, and such names clearly attest to Viking development of the town.

The Hiberno-Norse

Historically, the Viking settlement of Britain began around 874 after the initial overwintering at Torksey on the River Trent on the present Nottinghamshire and Lincolnshire border. From here, eventually, the three large Viking blocs of East Anglia, the north-east Midlands and York emerged. This is documented by the *Anglo-Saxon Chronicles*, but they omit another group of 'Scandinavian' settlers which did have an impact on the upland areas of the southern Pennine fringes. This secondary Anglo-Scandinavian settlement, which occurred on these more-marginal lands during the tenth century (see, for example, Hodges, 1989, p.64; Gelling, 1992, p.130), is usually referred to as 'Hiberno-Norse'. As the name might suggest, the Hiberno-Norse came to the region largely from Ireland via north Wales and the Wirral. They have almost evaded the histories, probably because their political impact was largely insignificant to the West Saxons.

Around 902, a group of Norse Vikings apparently settled, by permission of the Anglo-Saxon Mercians, around Chester after, according to English and Irish texts, they were expelled from Dublin (Gelling, 1992, p.130). This Norse, or more specifically Hiberno-Norse, settlement in north-western England appears to have coincided with a time when, in north-west Mercia, the West Saxons and their Mercian allies were beginning to conquer land from the Vikings. The Norse group, or groups, were allowed to remain, simply because they were adept at utilizing the more-marginal landscapes of the large estates in the region, and in the Chester area we know that they made use of the poorly-drained farmland of the Wirral (*ibid.*, p.130; Griffiths, 2001, p.179). Chester seems to have been the administrative centre for a large area (possibly that of the former *Wreocansaetna*), much larger than the present-day county of Cheshire, also including Manchester, which was annexed from the York Vikings in 919.

One of these groups of Hiberno-Norse people are known to have settled somewhere to the east of Manchester (Gelling, 1992, p.130; Hodges, 1991, p.116), taking advantage of the little-used Pennine slopes. However, as we are sometimes reminded (for example O'Sullivan, 1992), the term 'Hiberno-Norse' should not be regarded as a statement of racial origin, and indeed Downham finds the idea of a definite Hiberno-Norse identity 'particularly troublesome' (Downham, 2009, p.141). It is better seen – as it is meant here – as a broad term for those settling in England during the tenth century from origins in the British west. These settlers may have included a 'mixed bag' of identities, including groups of Welsh, Irish or others who were perhaps not strictly 'Norse' at all, but they did all share a common purpose and used their abilities to develop the more marginal land around the southern Pennines (see Hodges, 1989, p.64). However, place-name evidence from the Pennine uplands suggests that settlement there largely featured groups with a specifically Hiberno-Norse identity (Redmonds, 1988, p.3).

In the Peak District, or rather on its fringes, Hiberno-Norse settlement can be identified from name elements and decorated stone monuments with specific design attributes (see below). Because it seems that there was no direct Scandinavian occupation in most of the Peak District (Sidebottom, 2020, p.116), the presence of the Hiberno-Norse is more easily identified. Here, Norse settlement took advantage of the marginal areas of the large Peak District estates, areas where previous exploitation of the land was minimal on the gritstone valley slopes surrounding the limestone core. It was a symbiotic relationship, just as it had been in the Wirral, where the prosperity of the estate could be enhanced by farming the peripheral areas and increasing productivity.

In South and West Yorkshire, however, tenth-century Hiberno-Norse settlement is more difficult to identify; only name elements tell us of the presence of Norse settlers (Redmonds, 1988), and Faull and Moorhouse note (1981, p.197) that the same group or groups from the west, who originally settled in the Wirral, can be identified not only through place-names but also by feature-names in West Yorkshire. In addition to 'Norse' place-names (possibly in areas where Scandinavian settlement was relatively high) there was a large impact of the Scandinavian language on small-scale geographical features (individual fields, streams, copses, etc.) as an indicator that small-holding Old Norse speakers were living and farming in the countryside, not simply ruling from elite centres (Stattel, 2020, pp.4–5). A good example is the area of woodland called Grimbocar, close to the village of Derwent on the present Derbyshire–Yorkshire border; clearly a name of Scandinavian derivation, even though the village place-name is not Scandinavian. Close by, a cross shaft of

'Norse' design was found in the ruins of the old Derwent village, now inundated by the Ladybower Reservoir (Sidebottom, 1993).

This is not to say that there was no continuing immigration by Scandinavians throughout the late Saxon period. Abrams and Parsons (2004) conclude that many Scandinavian landholdings in marginal locations suggest low-status settlers, and that many of the place-names were coined right up to the eleventh century. Although settlement in the hillsides of South and West Yorkshire by the Hiberno-Norse perhaps began with a relatively sudden influx during the early-tenth century, it appears to have been part of a continuing Scandinavian immigration from elsewhere in the Viking world, which lasted through the late-Saxon period and beyond. Documentary evidence for this is poor, to say the least, and the archaeological evidence is difficult to identify, largely because of the high degree of acculturation that appears to have taken place. Place-names do, however, support an expanding Scandinavian-stimulated settlement over time. Some Scandinavian name elements do not show themselves until after the *Domesday* survey in 1086; for example, Herringthorpe near Rotherham, Jordanthorpe or Waterthorpe near Sheffield, and Netherthorpe, Cutthorpe or Woodthorpe in north-east Derbyshire. Interestingly, this lack of *Domesday* entries includes all of the '...thorpe' names south of the River Don in South Yorkshire (Williams and Martin, 1992). What can be said is that many of the hillslope settlements of South Yorkshire seem to owe their origins to Norse immigration, either directly from Scandinavia or otherwise.

Chapter 8

The 'New' Mercian–Northumbrian Boundary

'Yet Yorkshiremen who insist on their peculiar identity will be disconcerted to find that the southern boundary of their county has not been a permanent fixture over the centuries. The border fluctuated during the conflicts between Mercia and Northumbria in ways that are not clear.' (David Hey, 2000, p.31)

Despite limited settlement in the region, the Scandinavian presence in southern Yorkshire did have a major impact on the landscape, especially south of the River Don and in neighbouring north-east Derbyshire. The Viking annexation of much of Northumbria (developing into a new polity based on *Jorvik*) and north-eastern Mercia led to a new extension of geographical control for the York Vikings which eventually became formulized in a boundary similar to that between the later counties of Yorkshire and Derbyshire, the latter first mentioned in the eleventh century. In 942, the *Anglo-Saxon Chronicles* inform us that Viking York's control reached as far 'as Dore and Whitwell Gap the boundary form and Humber River, that broad ocean-stream' (Garmonsway, 1953, pp.110–11). The term 'Humber River' probably referred not only to the Humber estuary but also that area of marsh and lowland – the Humberhead Levels – which included the lower reaches of the Don and the marshland surrounding the River Idle and formed the eastern boundary at this point. The Dore–Whitwell line of demarcation has often been taken to be an ancient boundary (see Hey, 2000), largely because it is the only boundary between the two kingdoms that has ever been documented. However, the entry in the *Chronicles* suggest that this was a new boundary which needed to be described in the landscape rather than one already established that did not need to be.

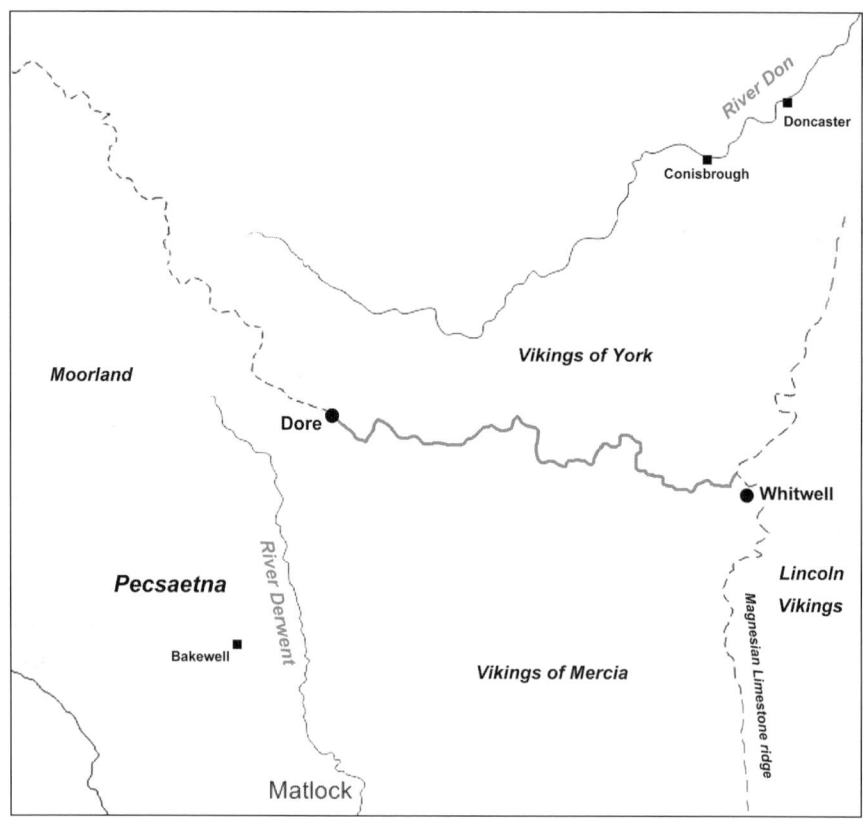

Fig. 26: 'The new border'.

The southward shift of boundary meant that Doncaster was no longer in the frontier zone between Northumbria and Mercia; now there was an entirely new order in the region. The borderland of South Yorkshire was now between two Viking groups, those taking control of north-eastern Mercia and those of Viking York. That is not to say that these two groups were one and the same, but they had evolved control in England out of an agreement between allies, probably following the overwintering at Repton (see Biddle and Kjolbye-Biddle, 1992). The tentative archaeological evidence at Doncaster suggests that during the tenth century, it became a town (a *burh*) on the Great North Road (Parker, 1987, pp.31–32; Hey, 2003, p.27), rather than simply a fortified refuge as it probably was before. This change of status for Doncaster led to new landholdings emerging in its hinterland, as discussed further below, but first it is worth examining the background to this new frontier.

Dore and Whitwell

Before the Scandinavian settlement of the ninth century, Dore is mentioned in the *Anglo-Saxon Chronicles* for the year 829. The event is now commemorated by a stone, erected on Dore village green, declaring that, in this year, the king of Northumbria submitted to the West Saxon ruler, Ecgbert. King Ecgbert, with the support of the East Angles, had exploited a power vacuum in Mercia and seized control of it, amassing a large army and seeking to gain tribute (payment in kind) from the Northumbrians. However, this West Saxon supremacy was short-lived, as the *Chronicles* entry for the next year (830) mentions, in a single line of text, that Wiglaf (king of Mercia) regained his kingdom (Garmonsway, 1953, pp.60, 110). No other information was given and one suspects this lack of detail was to underplay a rather ignominious West Saxon defeat by the Mercians, now under a single and powerful leader. From then onwards, West Saxon influence in the region was extinguished for the better part of 100 years.

The location of the Dore stone is almost certainly in the wrong place (see Sidebottom, 2020). The Dore – meaning a gateway or (literally) a door – mentioned in the *Chronicles* refers to what became known as Dore Moor, some 2km or so north-west of the village centre, in particular where a Roman road passed through it (Welsh, 1984; Sidebottom, 2020, pp.76–81). This road linked the forts at *Navio* (Brough-on-Noe), now in north Derbyshire, with those at Templeborough and *Danum* (Doncaster). At this point the road seemingly passed through a boundary (hence the name), yet this was not an established one between the kingdoms of Mercia and Northumbria, but the north-eastern limits of the land unit of the *Pecsaetna*, who primarily occupied the limestone Peak District as it is known today. The choice of Dore by the West Saxons in 829 tells us two things. Firstly, it reveals that the *Pecsaetna* land unit was under the control of the Mercians and thus part of the land taken over in turn by the West Saxons; indeed, we know that in 835 the Mercians had documented interests in the Peak and its lead production (Hart, 1975, p.102), so this is not an unreasonable assumption. Secondly, it would seem that much of South Yorkshire was then under Northumbrian control, and presumably Elmet as well. However, we cannot say that Dore was actually on the Northumbrian boundary at this time. All we can say is that it was probably somewhere within sight of the West Saxon army amassed on Dore Moor, but this could have been just about anywhere to the north and east of it, including the hills to the north of the River Don where the fortifications were located. The next mention of Dore, in 942, was after the Viking conquest, and during the Viking period the Peak seems to have been devoid of Scandinavian settlement, being controlled – at least by the tenth century – by an Anglo-Saxon, Uhtred (Sidebottom, 2020, pp.111–20; Sawyer, 1975, p.33). In that case, the West Saxon army did not have to pass through Viking-controlled territory until this point in the landscape at Dore.

The significance of Dore was its vantage point: the Roman road rose to a high point overlooking the Limb Valley on the western edge of the city of Sheffield, around 400 metres above sea level, with extensive views over land to the north and north-east. This was much higher than the earthworks at the southern end of Elmet – the Roman Rig (discussed below) – which stand little more than 100 metres above sea level, and Dore Moor can be seen clearly from there. Doncaster was also in view from here, as well as the Don and Idle lowlands, the border with *Haethfelthlund* and, in the far distance, the Trent Valley and the limestone escarpment beyond it on which now stands Lincoln Cathedral. Approximately 1km to the south-east of the Roman road, archaeological investigations have identified what has been interpreted as a Roman signal station, standing on the same ridge of land by Limb Brook (Waddington, 2017), suggesting that this has long been regarded as a highpoint that overlooked a sensitive area. To the north of the signal station, and less than 300 metres from the Roman road, is an undated earthwork which has yet to be investigated. It is known as Castle Dyke and has the appearance of an Iron Age hillfort with a section of double ditch and bank facing the projected line of the Roman road. It occupies an area of some 27 hectares and could have been used, or reused (if it had Iron Age origins), as an encampment by a significant army. An army massed at this vantage point would have been seen from afar, presenting a formidable presence on the skyline.

If the West Saxon army occupied the high ground overlooking the Don Valley and beyond, where was the Northumbrian army stationed? There are three probabilities. They could have been stationed along the Roman Rig earthworks to the north-east or

Fig. 27: The Dore stone.

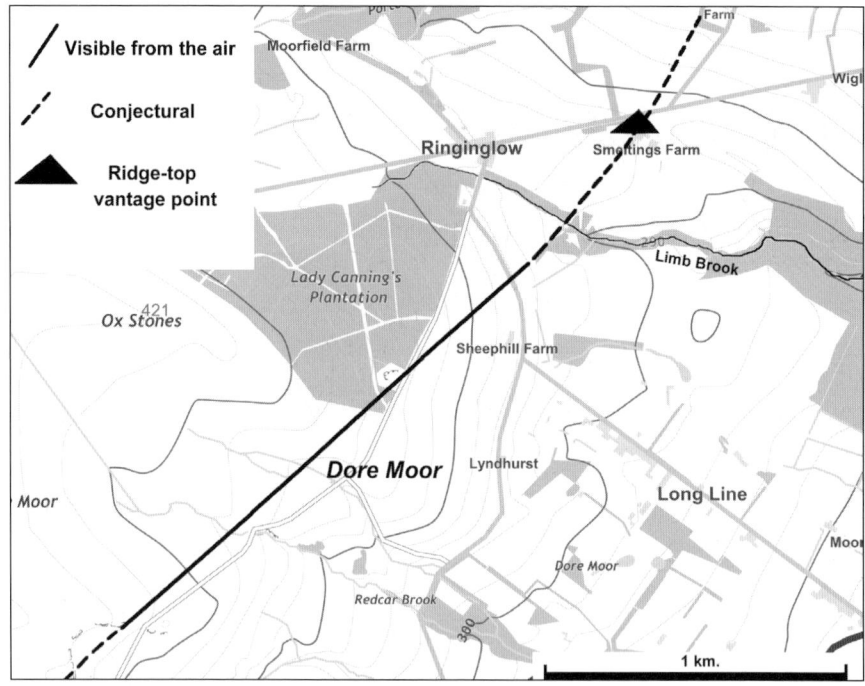

Fig. 28: The Houndkirk Roman Road (Opendata map).

Fig. 29: The vista from Dore Moor.

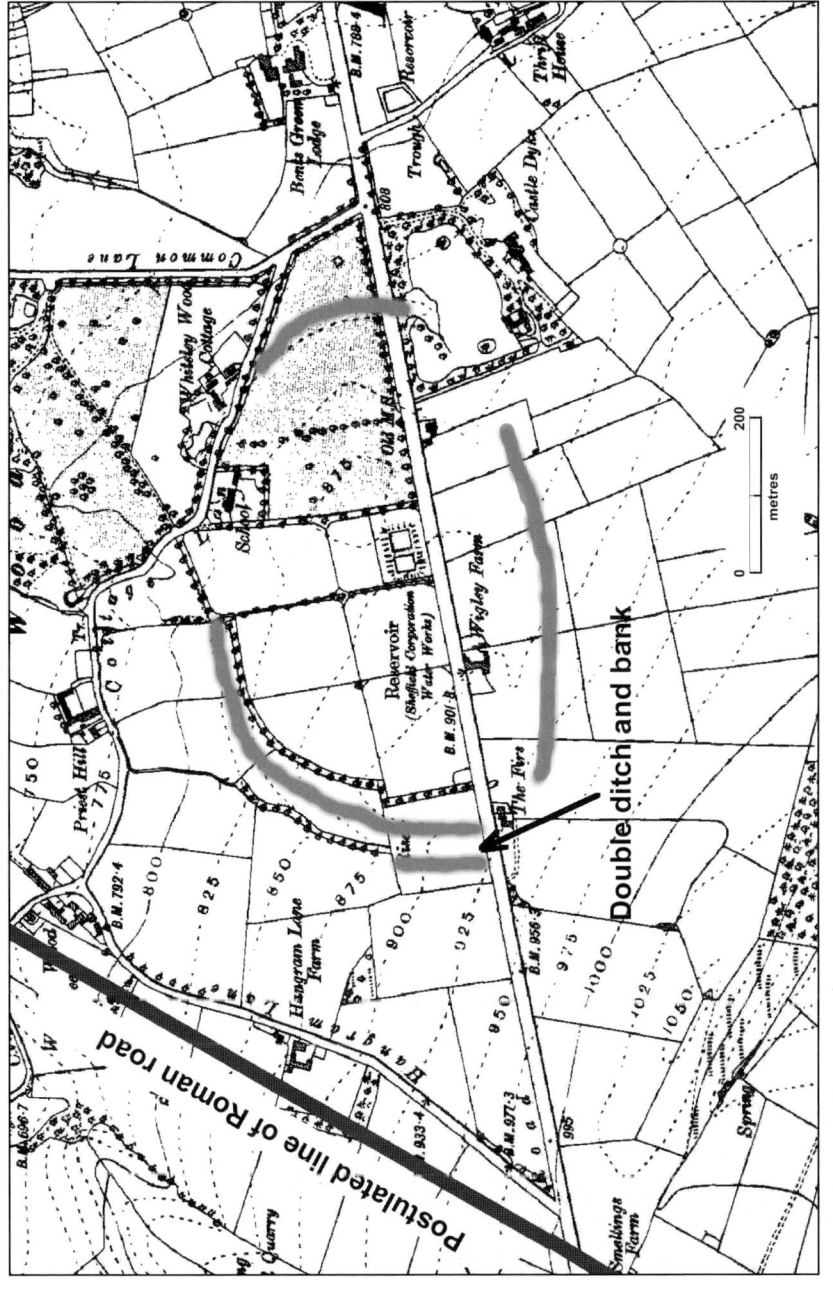

Fig. 30: Castle Dyke earthworks (based on Ordnance Survey, 1924).

even along the Bar Dyke earthworks to the north. Both were, and are, visible from Dore Moor, but perhaps the distances involved for these two locations would have been too far to demonstrate the size and organization of the respective armies. So it is possible that the Northumbrian army was considerably closer, and given that the most probable route taken by them would have been along the Roman road from Templeborough, they could have been deployed along the north side of the Porter Brook valley. The most likely high-point on that side of the Porter valley would have been roughly where the present Fulwood Church now stands.

In the entry in the *Chronicles* for 829, only Dore is mentioned as a boundary point. However, when it is mentioned again in 942, after the Viking settlement, we see that it is in association with Whitwell Gap (Garmonsway, 1953, p.110). Assuming that this is the Whitwell now in north Derbyshire, the 'gap' may refer to the dry limestone valley that passes through the Magnesian Limestone ridge at this point or, perhaps less likely, a cleared area through part of what was later known as Sherwood Forest. That Whitwell is identified as a significant boundary point in 942 suggests that land to the east of it was under separate jurisdiction, and this appears to have been that of the Lincoln Vikings. The distribution of Viking-period stone monuments certainly suggests that this was so, as discussed below. Whitwell stands on the Magnesian Limestone ridge, which extends southwards as far as Broxstowe, now in Nottinghamshire, and this may have formed the boundary between the Lincoln Vikings and those of north-eastern Mercia, as well as serving a similar function before the Viking settlement. The development of extensive woodland extending eastwards from the Magnesian Limestone, later known as Sherwood Forest, was probably more to do with political separation than anything else. Here, the soils and underlying geology make for prime agricultural land, so woodland regeneration after the collapse of the Roman economy was unlikely to have resulted from seeking better farmland elsewhere. One further reason why Whitwell was regarded as a significant place in the post-Viking world was that it was located adjacent to the traceable southern end of Ryknield Street (Hey, 2003, pp.16–17), which seems to have played a role in early Viking settlement, as outlined above, and provided a communication route to the north. It is perhaps worth mentioning that the Magnesian Limestone escarpment would also have been visible in the distance from the standpoint at Dore Moor.

In 942, therefore, there was a line of demarcation in the landscape which separated Yorkshire (the jurisdiction of the kingdom of York) from the north Midlands, now subsumed into a conquered Mercia and under West Saxon control by then. Once again, the land unit of the *Pecsaetna* had been used as a routeway through which the West Saxons had been able to directly confront the armies to the north, avoiding the Coal Measures landscape of north-east Derbyshire and South Yorkshire. Whether the new boundary line between Dore and Whitwell was one established between the York Vikings and the West Saxons in the mid-tenth century, or whether it already existed between the two Viking groups after the overwintering of the Vikings at Repton in 874, is unknown. However, the new boundary followed little more than an arbitrary line of minor watercourses. It is not certain that the county boundary preserved the exact line

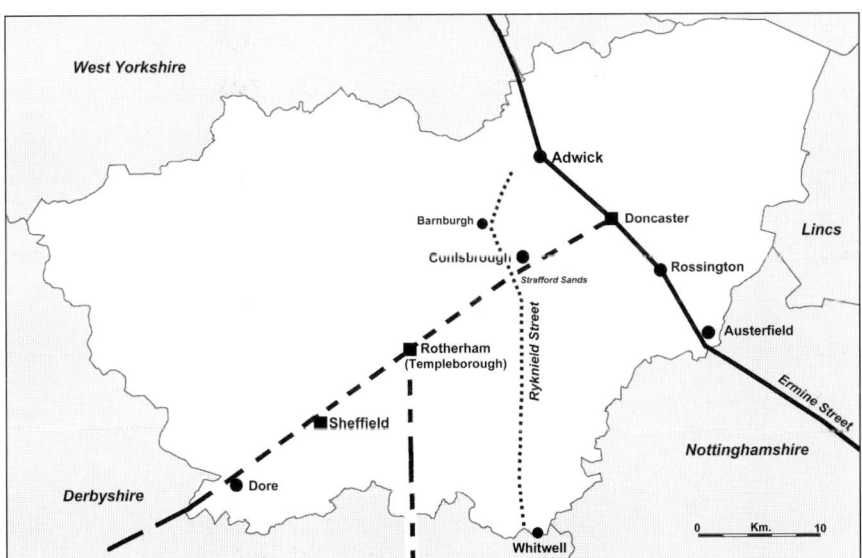

Fig. 31: Roman roads with Ryknield Street and Whitwell.

noted in 942, but no obvious alternatives to the present boundary exist (Hey, 2000, pp.37–39). In the west, Limb Brook, part of the River Sheaf and Meers Brook were used; further east, a portion of the River Rother and the County Dyke and Boundhay Dyke, provided the demarcation. None of these streams and minor rivers presented a formidable barrier, so they were no doubt chosen because they were recognized landscape features rather than defensive obstacles. This suggests that, on balance, the 'new' border may well have been formed between the two Viking factions, and probably by agreement, around the beginning of the tenth century.

It is likely that the mid-tenth century saw significant development in the region which now encompasses north-east Derbyshire and South Yorkshire south of the River Don. Before then, it appears that there was little in the way of settlement, the region having given way to a considerable regeneration of woodland following the collapse of the Roman economy. Jones (1993, pp.9–12) highlights the large

Fig. 32: Limb Brook at Whirlow, Sheffield.

amount of woodland in the Sheffield region that developed during the post-Roman period and still survived into the late-medieval era. As an area of contention between Northumbria and Mercia in the pre-Viking period, South Yorkshire south of the Don did not offer any stability of tenure and, in short, had the potential to become a war zone at any moment. The archaeological record is almost silent for this period and we are reliant on indirect evidence such as place-name analysis. Documentary sources are equally elusive until the *Domesday* survey of 1086, when we are presented with a snapshot of landholdings and principal centres in the mid-eleventh century. There are, however, a few charters for the area which have an interesting distribution and are discussed below. Another form of evidence is that derived from carved stone monuments erected in the tenth century (see below). These seem to present another snapshot, but for a slightly earlier time, and like the later *Domesday* account offer an insight into local centres of control.

Chapter 9

Words, Names and Ethnicity in the Landscape

We have already seen how place-name evidence suggests a mix of Northumbrian and Mercian name-forms in southern Yorkshire, which argues for a surprisingly strong Mercian presence in the region. There are other place-names which indicate some territorial division. In particular, these are the 'in Elmet' names, which include Sherburn-in-Elmet, Barwick-in-Elmet and Saxton-in-Elmet, along with five other examples, as well as the mysterious 'Alta Methelton in Elmete' found in a thirteenth-century document. The latter may well have been High Melton, which is just to the north of Conisbrough in South Yorkshire. There is another fourteenth-century record referring to the 'Towne of Kirkeby in Elmet', which is now known as South Kirkby (Jones, 1975, p.15). The 'in-Elmet' names need not be particularly ancient; the Elmet that appears to be delineated by them may not be the same as the original 'kingdom' mentioned by Bede in the seventh century. One of the 'in-Elmet' names – 'Kirkeby' – is clearly Scandinavian, so it is difficult to see 'in-Elmet' as evidence for a particularly ancient boundary marker, although it may well have existed by the tenth century.

The distribution of the names tends to show that Elmet was regarded as to the north of the River Don, which is coterminous with a land unit that may at some time have been protected by the Roman Rig earthworks, Doncaster and the fortified *burhs*. They all share a specific positioning in the landscape in that they follow a distinct geological north–south line, shadowing the Magnesian Limestone ridge, which could be taken as the eastern boundary of Elmet; and of course the Roman road of Ermine Street also followed this ridge (see Fig. 33). Interestingly, the few Anglo-Saxon pagan burials in the region are all to the east of this line (see earlier discussion and, for example, Faull and Moorhouse, 1981), so the 'in-Elmet' names may well be describing a boundary that has its roots even further into antiquity.

We have previously discussed the Mercian input into southern Yorkshire and how this is reflected, *inter alia*, in the inclusion of the *Elmedsaetna* in the *Tribal Hidage* tribute list. Kolb's dialect studies (1973) have also identified areas of southern Yorkshire which seem to have a specific linguistic identity. Whereas some dialects were found to be widespread, spanning almost all of the West Riding, others appear to have a distinct boundary within the county or are confined to a specific area where particular dialectic sounds are prevalent and geographically isolated. Kolb identifies 'ate', 'stole', 'spoke' and 'rode' dialect forms which are only found between an area of the

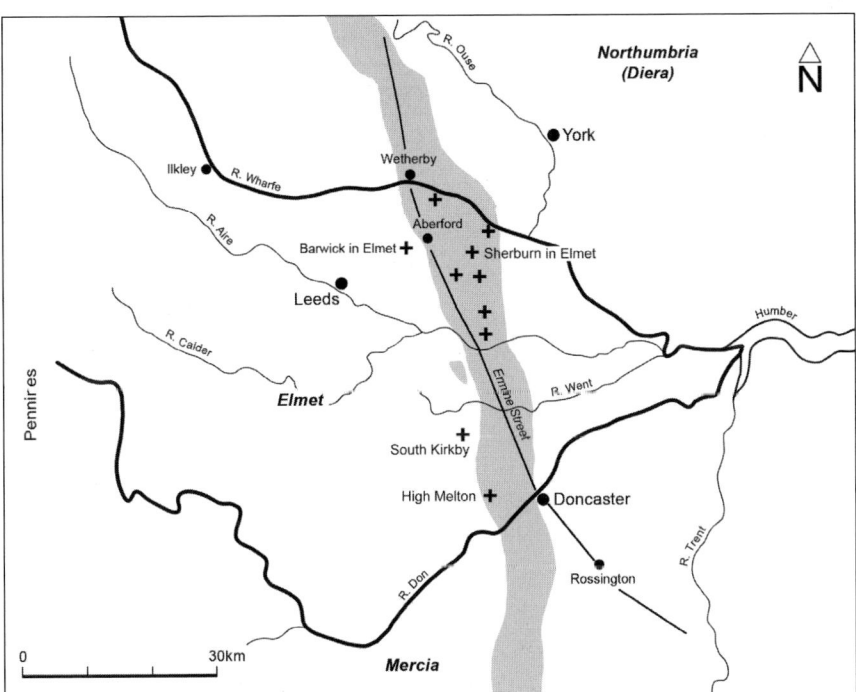

Fig. 33: 'In-Elmet' place-names (based on Jones, 1975, and Loveluck, 2003).

upper Don Valley in the region of Penistone and north of the Calder Valley around Huddersfield (Kolb, 1973, p.302). This, incidentally, is also defined by a particular group of stone monuments dating to the later-Saxon period (see 'Anglo-Saxon Stone Monuments in South Yorkshire' chapter below). One possible reason for this highly-localized set of dialectic properties is the hillslope settlement by incomers from the tenth century onwards – the Hiberno-Norse – discussed earlier. There are also a few dialectic sounds which see the middle Don Valley as its northern boundary. These include what Kolb terms the 'goose', 'school', 'tooth' and 'foot' dialect words which extend from the southern West Riding boundary down to the north Midlands, including the present city of Sheffield (Kolb, 1973, pp.303–07). This, however, is a small area of South Yorkshire and it is not unreasonable to expect some transmission of dialectic forms across a county boundary which presents no geological or topographical obstacles.

'Eccles' and the British connection

Place-name analysis in the old West Riding has shown that there are a substantial number of British names, mostly containing the elements 'walh', 'brettas', 'cumbra' and 'eccles', as well as 'Welsh' names which have 'survived in an English guise' (Gruffydd, 1994, p.67), side-by-side with Anglo-Saxon names. Names that have a British origin are found throughout England, but rarely on the scale that they are in the old West Riding of Yorkshire (see Fig. 35). Higham (1993a, p.101) notes that by the late Saxon period, British place-names were so rare that they identified communities that were residual Britons, but the lack of Germanic material culture in southern Yorkshire suggests that Britons here were more than residual.

The name element 'eccles', as in place-names such as Ecclesfield or Ecclesall, is usually taken to refer to a location where a church was already established by the time Anglo-Saxon became the dominant language. It is a term borrowed from Latin that was used in the so-called 'Celtic' areas of western Britain to describe a Christian church. For example, the Primitive Welsh element is *'egles'*, whilst *'eglos'* is found in Cornwall and *'eglis'* or *'eclis'* in Old Irish (Cameron, 1975a, p.1). However, the origin of some, or all, of the 'eccles' place-name elements may not be that simple, and it is pertinent that *ecclesia* is Latin and neither an Anglo-Saxon, nor a British term. There is a concentration of 'eccles' name-elements around the Peak District and in South Yorkshire. They occur, for example, at Ecclesall and Ecclesfield (now parts of Sheffield), Eccles House (near Hope), Eccles House and Eccles Pike (near Chapel-en-le-Frith) and Ecclesbourne Brook (near Wirksworth), while Hart (1981, p.117) makes a case for Eagle Tor (formerly Eccles Tor) near Stanton-in-the-Peak to be included in this list. Further afield, they are also found in West Yorkshire and in Pennine Lancashire, near Manchester.

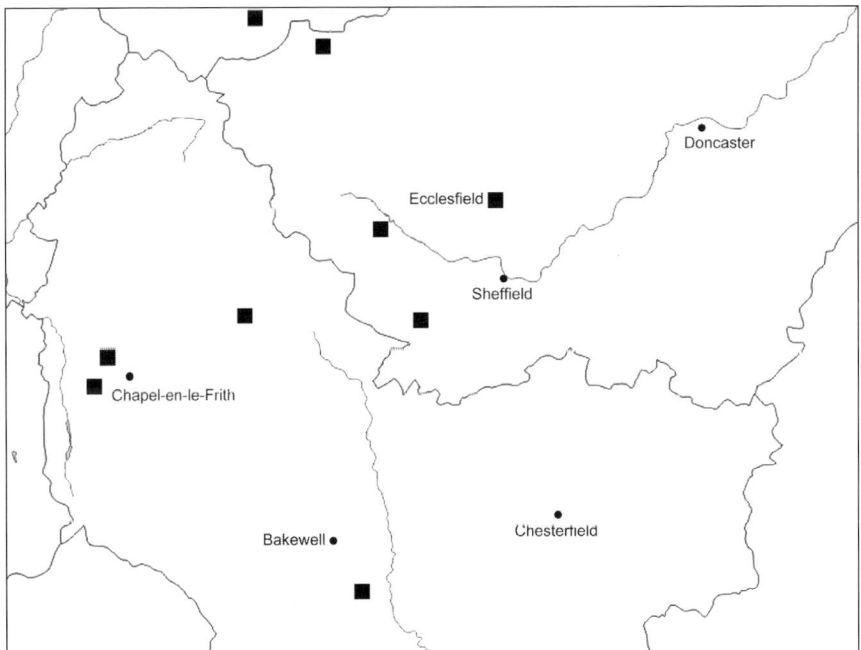

Fig. 34: 'Eccles' place-names (based on Hart, 1981, and Higham, 1993a).

The distribution of 'eccles' name-elements does, therefore, have a specific geography. Cameron (1975b, pp.4–6) says that they are concentrated in western-central England, and notes that Faull adds that they occupy sites found on fairly steep hillsides and are often close to parish or old estate boundaries (ibid., p.6). It is particularly interesting that all of the 'eccles' name-elements in Yorkshire are confined to the former British kingdom of Elmet (Faull and Moorhouse, 1981, p.175), assuming this to be largely the same as the former West Riding of Yorkshire. Taylor's study in this area shows that 'eccles' name-elements are found to coincide with a high number of other British name-elements such as 'bretta', 'cumbra' and 'walh' (see below). As in 'Ecclesfield', they are invariably hybridized with Anglo-Saxon elements such as '*feld*' or '*tun*'. These particular British elements, he suggests, may indicate pockets of native inhabitants surviving under an overall Anglo-Saxon administration (Taylor, 1992), but it is argued here that their survival could also be indicative of more than just 'pockets' of native population in areas where Anglo-Saxon settlement was severely limited.

The survival of British name-elements can also be linked to topography. None of them occupy prime agricultural land, instead being found on poorer soils in areas that may be considered marginal in terms of agricultural value (Taylor, 1992) and not somewhere of prime interest to the Anglo-Saxon overlords of Elmet and surrounding Pennine districts. Notably, 'eccles' name-elements are not found in the East Midlands (Cameron, 1975, p.4), nor in the Vale of York (Faull and Moorhouse, 1981, p.175), where there is good arable land and archaeological evidence for primary Anglo-Saxon settlement. In contrast, as we have discussed, evidence for 'ethnically' Anglo-Saxon settlement in the Pennine foothills of south-western Yorkshire is almost entirely absent (*ibid.*). Similarly, there is a group of 'eccles' name-elements to the west of the southern Pennines, an area where Anglo-Saxon settlement evidence is equally elusive. Almost none of the 'eccles' sites appears to have been located centrally to old estate units, but in their more peripheral areas. In other words, it is difficult to argue that, in following the usual pattern of estate formation, such sites were central to pre-Conquest administrative units (Jones, 1975, p.22). However, our knowledge of pre-Conquest estates is largely from the *Domesday* account and probably reflects a great deal of reorganization over the centuries. One exception appears to be Ecclesfield, which eventually became part of the 'shire' (a large pre-Conquest estate) of Hallamshire. Hey (2002, p.9) suggests that Ecclesfield was the estate centre until Sheffield grew to prominence in much later times (see also Parker, 1985), although Ecclesfield, in turn, may once have been just a part of a much larger administrative unit. It is perhaps the 'eccles' name, or rather the interpretation of its meaning, that has led to the idea that Ecclesfield was a centre of considerable antiquity (see, for example, Hey, 2003, p.22), but given the possible alternative and later origin of the name-element (discussed below), there is no evidence to suppose that Ecclesfield was a particularly early centre.

We have already discussed the likelihood of a long-term survival of a British administration in southern and western Yorkshire, where the lack of Anglo-Saxon material culture evidence corresponds to an abundance of British place-name elements. All of this provides an indication that 'eccles' place-names may not be as ancient as previously supposed. The evidence for Christianity in Roman Britain is slight, largely being confined to the dwellings of the elite. It was not the official religion of the Empire until the fourth century, a time when Roman authority in Britain was waning. There was probably less Roman cultural influence in *Britannia Secunda*, particularly in areas marginal to Roman interests such as the southern Pennines. So churches as we know them in these areas were probably not established before the major Anglo-Saxon kingdoms had developed and a new phase of church-building had resulted from the spread of Christian dioceses associated with the large kingdoms. These were likely to have been promoted by the new Anglo-Saxon overlords, especially after the introduction of the Roman Church during the seventh century. In areas like southern Yorkshire where there is a particular concentration of British name-elements – and where there were no doubt corresponding native dialects which included words not used by the Germanic incomers – the native population was likely to have been instrumental in the formation of local place-names, as suggested for Ecclesfield. The distribution of 'eccles' names, therefore, probably reflects no more than the history and application of local linguistics. Since a British administration survived in Elmet at least until the seventh century, and possibly for longer, the localized usage of the term 'eccles' may have been perpetuated right into the later Anglo-Saxon period.

There is another reason why 'eccles' names may have crept into the southern Pennine landscape; odd though it might seem, it is due to a 'Scandinavian' input by way of the Hiberno-Norse. We have already discussed that the Hiberno-Norse came to Pennine areas during the early tenth century, and we know that they settled and farmed in the upland areas of southern Yorkshire. Such a pattern of secondary settlement is also suggested for those areas where 'eccles' name-elements are found, on the poorer soils and on the fringes of established estates. By the tenth century, many Hiberno-Norse were likely to be second or even third-generation expatriates of the British West, and their name for a Christian church is more likely to have been one used by British-speaking inhabitants rather than that used by the Anglo-Saxons. If a large number of the southern Pennine population was also British-speaking, then British words – such as 'eglos', for example – were likely to be reinforced by these linguistic influences from elsewhere. Interestingly, one of the four previous landholders in Ecclesfield mentioned in the *Domesday* survey was still known as 'Northmann' (Williams and Martin, 1992, p.829).

'Eccles' is not the only British name-element in southern Yorkshire. There are a number of others, largely including the elements 'walh', 'brettas' and 'cumbra' (Faull and Moorhouse, 1981, p.175). 'Wala' names refer to British settlements, for example Walton, Walsden, Walshaw and Wadsworth, although, as noted earlier, some 'Wal' examples may refer to the Mercian element *'waella'* (stream) or '*wald*' (wood), or even '*wall*' (meaning wall). However. Faull and Moorhouse (1981, pp.175–76) consider many of them to be early names, including Walton near Cleckheaton in West Yorkshire, where a large cross base (the 'Walton Cross') stands in a field (see also Coatsworth, 2008, pp.162–64). The 'brettas' place-names refer to Britons (as in Breton, Brittany), often compounded with an English element or even Scandinavian; good examples are West Bretton in West Yorkshire and Monk Bretton in South Yorkshire. 'Brettas' names are particularly prevalent in the valleys of the rivers Don and Aire (Faull, 1977). 'Cumbra' name elements have the same root as '*Cymry*' (meaning Welsh) and the same element is found in Cumbria and Cumberland; they are also found in the two Cumberworth place-names in southern Yorkshire.

Examination of Fig. 35, which shows the distribution of 'British' name-elements in South and West Yorkshire, reveals that they are

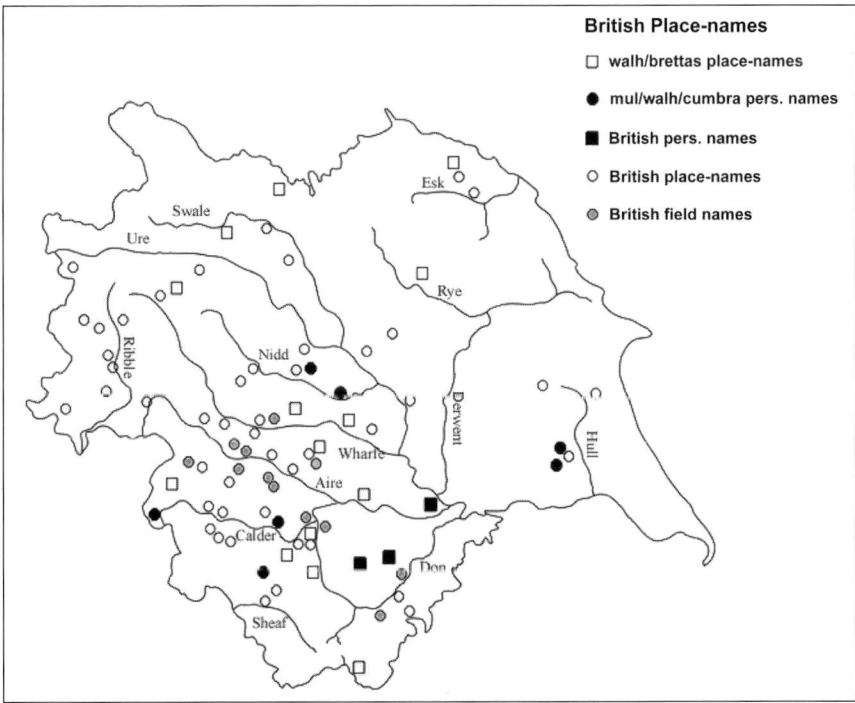

Fig. 35: British place-names (based on Faull, 1977).

concentrated in the river valleys of the old land unit of Elmet in West and South Yorkshire. Higham adds that similar evidence for British name elements presents itself in Pennine Lancashire (1993a, p.101), again areas where early Germanic settlement evidence is largely lacking. These are, of course, areas where existing native settlements are likely to have continued with minimal Anglo-Saxon infiltration, but where some input from Scandinavian settlers from the British West was also prevalent, adding to, and reinforcing, hybridization in the formation of place, field and landscape names.

Chapter 10

Anglo-Saxon Stone Monuments in South Yorkshire

Stone monuments as an artefact for examining regional identities

Throughout Yorkshire and the north Midlands, Anglo-Saxon decorated stone crosses have been found buried in the ground, reused in the fabric of churches or languishing in fields and churchyards. Only a very small number of them are anywhere near complete, the vast majority being fragments that have been reused as building lintels, quoins or simply part of wall-building. Despite the abundance of cross fragments across the north and Midlands, their origin is obscure. There is no documentary evidence for them and no cross can be demonstrated to have been found in its original context. As such, there are, not surprisingly, a number of problems with our basic understanding of them, not least what they were for or when were they erected, although their distribution and context suggests that they were to do with landholdings at a particular period in time. In this respect, they are a useful artefact from the pre-Conquest period and can inform us about centres of administration and political relationships. It will be useful to explain here how recent research has shown that the monuments are, in fact, political statements, and not simply artistic expression from the Anglo-Saxon period.

As far as their chronology is concerned, the lack of context makes this highly problematic. Almost no monument has been dated by archaeological means, with the few exceptions only able to provide a broad horizon spanning several centuries. For example, a cross shaft found at York during an archaeological excavation could only be dated by its archaeological context to sometime 'before AD 960' (Lang, 1991, p.104). The main problem is that once a monument is taken down or moved, it is immediately removed from its context; most were reused elsewhere or became buried in disturbed ground. To try to overcome this, a number of assumptions have been developed to try to explain their function and dating. However, these were first made over a century ago, and with little alternative evidence to offer, the fundamentals of these assumptions have stood largely unchallenged.

As many crosses have been found near, or in, churchyards, a strictly ecclesiastical context has always appeared reasonable, although many of these churches and churchyards cannot be dated to the pre-Conquest period. Evidence for pre-Conquest stone monuments being erected in the churchyard of a pre-existing church building is entirely lacking in many cases. For example, excavations at St Michael's Church in Workington (Cumbria) revealed extensive tenth-century sculptural remains, but despite extensive work at the site there was no shred of evidence that the earliest phase of the church building was older than the twelfth century (McCarthy and Paterson, 2014, p.128). The church was not recorded in the *Domesday* survey; in fact, Workington itself failed to be included (Williams and Martin, 1992). On the other hand, the archaeological evidence shows that the church of St Wystan at Repton in Derbyshire was already established by the time that sculptural monuments were erected there (see Biddle and Biddle, 1992). So the erection of stone monuments sometimes corresponded to the presence of a church building and sometimes not. The most likely explanation for this phenomenon is that they were erected in locations that once served as estate centres, or at least as some form of central place in terms of localized control. A few of these centres had churches, but others – perhaps most of them – did not.

The traditional dating of Anglo-Saxon stone sculpture fundamentally relies on an archaic notion of evolving art styles from the mid-eighth century through to the Norman Conquest, a model which rests on no evidence at all. The stylistic dating method was based on the belief that social evolution and periodic moral decadence would manifest itself through the styling and quality of carvings. This hypothesis proposed that early carvings were well executed, whereas later ones showed 'degeneration' and were of lesser accomplishment; this was described well by the antiquarian W.G. Collingwood (1854–1932):

> 'The normal trend of development is from severe design, naturalistic intention, and careful execution to … a greater show of clever handling. When this has reached its climax, decadence sets in with carelessness in touch and cheapness in design … And when the worst has come, some new impulse from without transforms the whole art … This is the history of the Anglian monuments, parallel to the history of the Anglian people.' (Collingwood, 1921, pp.20–21).

The stylistic dating method was developed when Darwin's evolutionary paradigm was being applied almost universally to past behaviour. This chronological sequencing, by the nature of any art history, needs a protracted period to demonstrate its progression, so dates have been assigned between the eighth and eleventh centuries, based simply on how a monument looks. This does not consider that different decorative styles may be due to alternative reasons, nor that available wealth (or lack of it) to commission and execute carvings could vary from location to location. Given the particular lack of evidence for the erection of crosses, especially in the region under discussion, Coatsworth (2008), in the national *Corpus of the Anglo-Saxon Stone Sculpture*, has dated South and West Yorkshire monuments art-historically using largely the method that was developed by Collingwood and his contemporaries all those years ago. Coatsworth's dates for the monuments range between the later ninth and tenth centuries, with only fragments at Darfield tentatively dated a little earlier; the latter may, however, have been architectural fragments rather than parts of freestanding crosses (Coatsworth, 2008, pp.127–28).

There are more inscriptions on stone cross shafts in the Yorkshire Pennines than anywhere else in England. Most of these are at Thornhill near Dewsbury on the south bank of the River Calder, where there are four separate runic inscriptions in Old English; they are quite interesting in terms of the possible function of the monuments. One cross shaft bears the legend 'Eþelbercht set up [this memorial] in memory of Eþelwini', while two other shafts have the inscriptions 'after Osberht, a beacon' and 'Eadred set up [this monument] in memory of Eateinne'. All these inscriptions, and indeed the standard formula across northern England, suggest succession – 'erected by x, after y', showing the present tenant of a landholding has an ancestral claim to it. But perhaps the most instructive inscription at Thornhill reads 'Gilswith raised up after Berhtswith, a beacon on a hill [or mound]; pray for her soul' (D. Parsons in Coatsworth, 2008, pp.79–84). The mention of a beacon on a mound (or hill) suggests that the cross was not originally in a churchyard or within a church building, but in a prominent position in the landscape. This kind of setting is far from unique; just over the Pennines at Cleulow in Cheshire, for example, a round-sectioned cross shaft stands on a prominent hill overlooking the surrounding landscape, far away from any possible ecclesiastical setting (Sidebottom, 1994, p.153). Similar comments apply to the so-called 'Pillar of Eliseg' in eastern Wales, which also stands on a mound and may not only have been a commemorative monument but also a regional meeting place (Williams, 2010, p.15); it is certainly not in an ecclesiastical setting.

The composition of Anglo-Saxon England was anything but uniform. Any notion of ubiquitous Anglo-Saxon and Anglo-Scandinavian design elements as stages of some sort of universal fashion expression were clearly undermined as we began to understand that even large and seemingly homogenous kingdoms such as Mercia or Northumbria were, in fact, an amalgam of disparate groups. It is

Fig. 36: The Cleulow cross. (Photo © Dave Dunford (cc-by-sa/2.0) and reproduced under Creative Commons licence)

also questionable that notions of 'period fashion' can be considered an appropriate concept in the minds of competitive 'tribal' groups of the mid- and later-Saxon periods, and it can now be shown that such chronological development is unlikely (Sidebottom, 1994 and 2000). In the north Midlands and southern Yorkshire at least, almost all monuments fall into the secular groupings that we can reconstruct with the aid of the *Tribal Hidage* and other documents. Where the *Tribal Hidage* fails to help us (as in the former kingdom of Northumbria), the distribution of Saxon-period stone monuments becomes all the more valuable. With careful examination, almost every monument can be seen to be identified, through its decoration, to a specific region with distinct geographical bounds (Sidebottom, 1994, 2000 and 2020). These groupings have been found to correspond with land divisions which were inherited, modified or created in the late Saxon period after the Viking settlement of the north Midlands (Hawkes and Sidebottom, 2018; Sidebottom, 2020) and southern Yorkshire (Sidebottom, 1994).

The monuments within each respective group share a common repertoire of design elements which give them their group characteristics and geographical integrity, which leads to the conclusion that all of them were likely to have been part of a synchronous phase of monumentation, rather than erected in chronological sequence. If the monuments had been produced over a period of time and subject to a continuing evolution of style, then this would have produced an array of loosely-defined (in a geographical sense) and differently-styled monuments, and it would therefore have been difficult, if not impossible, to identify specific design elements as being from a regional grouping, let alone any precise geographical region. It is clear that stylistic differences, then, are not due to temporal disparity, but to regional variation and that – certainly in the north Midlands – they can be related to various secular divisions that existed largely before, and certainly just after, the Viking settlement (Hawkes and Sidebottom, 2018; Sidebottom, 2000 and 2020). Furthermore, the distribution of almost all freestanding stone monuments in the wider region respects the historic extent of Viking settlement, whereas none are found to the south of the Viking annexation of northern Mercia, apart from a handful of outliers, most of which are coastal. From their national distribution, it thus seems more likely that they are all a Viking Age phenomenon; but the dating can be narrowed even further.

The leaders of the initial Viking settlement relied heavily on their relationship to 'pagan' deities, especially Odin (Woden), to legitimize their power. The Christian God was definitely the strict province of the Anglo-Saxon 'enemy'. Therefore, for the period after 876 and until Christianity was seen to be accepted by the northmen, we should not expect to see crosses raised in stone, especially in the vast quantity that survive even today. So we can ask the question: when were the Vikings (and other groups) likely to have needed to display such an overt acceptance of Christianity? The answer becomes apparent when we look at the submission process of the various groups of the north to the Anglo-Saxon kings of the south, in particular to the West Saxons. It is more than likely that the rationale behind the erection of the crosses was to acknowledge the overlordship of the West Saxon king and to recognize Christianity as a condition of settlement (Sidebottom, 1994 and 2000). The West Saxon kings had developed their administration on Frankish lines, where king and Church, in tandem, became the dominant power (Loyn, 1984, pp.82, 89); to submit to one, necessitated submission to the other. This is clearly seen in Guthrum's submission to Alfred in 878, where Christian baptism was a condition of Guthrum's continuing rule of East Anglia under West Saxon overlordship (ibid., p.62). The same conditions were presented to all of the northern groups (Viking and Anglo-Saxon) on a grand scale in 920; in fact, in all of the areas where freestanding stone monuments are found in abundance. In this respect, it is notable that no freestanding cross monuments have been discovered in the important pre-Viking Mercian centres of Stafford, Lichfield and Tamworth, which were outside the Viking-controlled north-east Midlands.

The submission statement is related in the *Anglo-Saxon Chronicles* (Garmonsway, 1953, p.104) when Edward of Wessex was proclaimed 'father and lord' (in the sense of godfather and overlord). Similar conditions appear to have been reinforced in around 926 when various Viking groups were again required to submit to Athelstan and were made to renounce 'idolatrous practices' (ibid., p.107). Although the *Chronicles* are silent on the mechanism by which the Vikings and other groups were supposed to demonstrate acknowledgement of their overlord and the Christian deity, the erection of stone crosses at their estate centres would seem highly appropriate. Therefore, many, if not all, of the freestanding monuments are likely to have been erected during a relatively short period of time, which was almost certainly during the first half of the tenth century (Sidebottom, 1994 and 2000). As such, their distribution can provide a valuable insight into settlement patterns and land control up to, and around, the early–mid-tenth century.

In the Midlands, we have a reasonable knowledge of land divisions from reconstructions of the *Tribal Hidage* (described above), which includes the smaller units which are otherwise poorly understood in territorial terms. From these reconstructions, it has been possible to identify regional groupings of stone monuments to those specific land divisions, such as those of the *Pecsaetna* (Sidebottom, 2020), the territories annexed by the Lincoln Vikings and Viking-controlled Mercia (Sidebottom, 1994 and 2000; Hawkes and Sidebottom, 2018). This is illustrated by Fig. 37, which also shows that a further group of monuments, with a different iconographic content to those elsewhere, can be identified to southern Yorkshire, presumably the land unit of the old kingdom of Elmet (from Sidebottom, 1994). Because the *Tribal Hidage* only included the *Elmedsaetna* in its list of land divisions north of the Midlands, it is has not been possible to carry the same exercise further north, where no documentary evidence exists for the small units that made up the larger kingdom of Northumbria.

There is also an array of stones that were erected by Hiberno-Norse settlers on the fringes of the large Peak estates (see Fig. 38). They can be identified by their iconographic content, which shares a commonality with stone monuments found in Cumbria, the Isle of Man and the Wirral (for discussion, see Bailey, 1980), and also by their geographic, topographic and geological locations, since they largely favoured the Gritstone margins of the limestone Peak District (Sidebottom, 2020, pp.58–69). Whilst we are fairly confident that these same Hiberno-Norse settlers also occupied enclaves in the upper reaches of the valleys of the Yorkshire Pennines (Faull and Moorhouse, 1981, p.197), their stone monuments are not so easily identified. Unlike the 'Norse' monuments in the Peak, the only tentative connection to topography and geology is that they are on, or close to, the Millstone Grit uplands of the western Yorkshire Pennines and form a cluster in the steeper valleys. Although they are less easy to identify, some design elements do suggest an affinity with those often associated with the Hiberno-Norse, but their iconographic identity appears to have become hybridized during the tenth century, making for a more localized set of design elements combining 'Norse', Anglo-Saxon and even western British characteristics. The

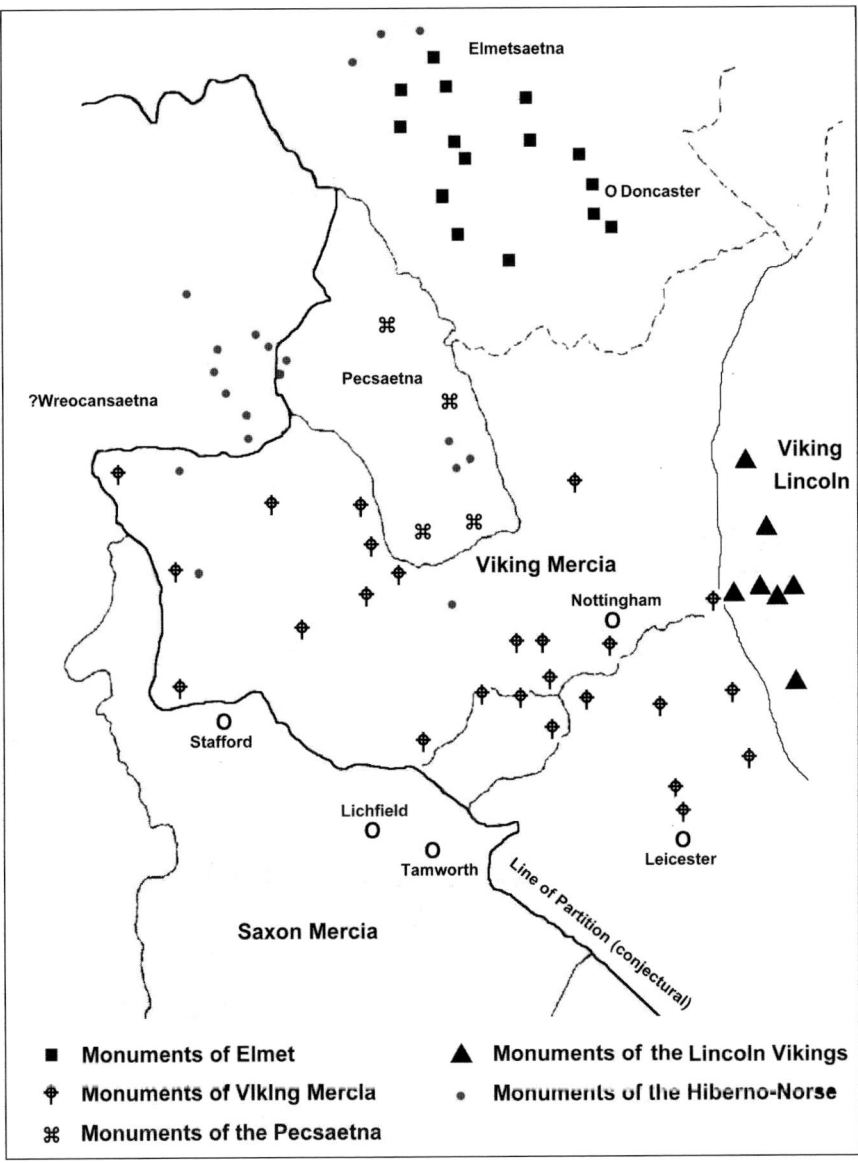

Fig. 37: Regional groups of monuments in the north Midlands and southern Yorkshire.

hybridization between Hiberno-Norse and other sculpture of the old West Riding was also noted by Coatsworth in the *Corpus of Anglo-Saxon Stone Sculpture* (2008, p.75).

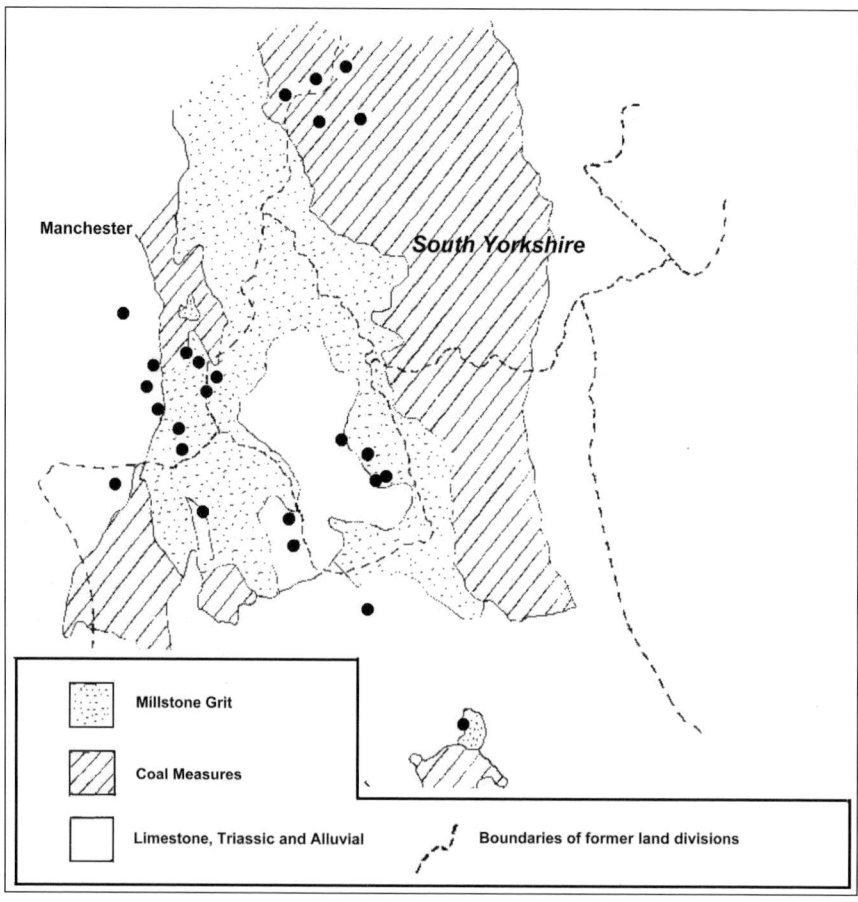

Fig. 38: 'Norse' monuments and geology.

In southern Yorkshire, three sites – at Birstall, Hartshead and Rastrick, all of which lie on the hillslopes in West Yorkshire (see Fig. 39) – may suggest a Hiberno-Norse presence more than others through their iconography, and they do seem to be in a topographical area where Hiberno-Norse settlement is to be expected. Interestingly, the three sites are roughly aligned to, and located just to the south of, the Roman road between Manchester and Tadcaster. The road appears to form the north-western boundary to a cluster of estates in this part of West Yorkshire and to demark the interface between the alluvial valleys of the rivers Calder and Aire and the higher ground of the Pennine 'tops'. The input of the Hiberno-Norse into Pennine settlement probably helped determine the way in which the area developed its iconographic elements to put on display and to distiguish it from the surrounding regions. This resulted in the monuments of South Yorkshire and southern West Yorkshire formimg an identifiable and geographically-coherant group when compared with monuments in the north Midlands and further afield. The sites where these monuments are displayed include Kirkburton, Kirkheaton, Thornhill and Dewsbury in southern West Yorkshire, and at Frickley, Cawthorne, Conisbrough, Mexborough, Penistone, Ecclesfield and High Hoyland in South Yorkshire (see Fig. 39). There is also a standing stone cross at Bradfield to the west of Sheffield, but this is difficult to identify to a regional group since it is largely devoid of decoration, but may well be from the Anglo-Saxon period (Sidebottom, 1994; Coatsworth, 2008, p.104). Similar comments apply to the probable double cross base at Bolsterstone (Coatsworth, 2008, p.274) which is undecorated (and possibly unfinished), but double cross bases do have parallels elsewhere, including that at Ecclesfield.

These carved stone monuments are, of course, known to us through discovery over the years, but it is likley that other sites may have existed where the monuments have been destroyed completely or have yet to be discovered. Nethertheless, the distribution of the known monument sites does tell us about the centres of estates that existed by the early–mid-tenth century in South Yorkshire; equally, they can tentatively identify those centres which developed later, simply by their absence, and we will return to this aspect of their distribution.

The iconographic attributes which are unique to southern West Yorkshire and South Yorkshire can be termed the Elmet Group (for want of a better term), since they seem to define at least the south-eastern part of Pennine Northumbria – under the control of the Vikings of York by the tenth century – of which Elmet seems to have been a significant part. The Elmet Group has three area-specific attributes which span the entire region. These overall signature decorative attributes (found together on the same pieces of sculpture, except where they are too fragmentary) present themselves, as one might say, as a 'package' which is easily recognizable in the same way that other groups outside this region in the north Midlands have their own identifiable design elements. The attributes are shared across the stone monuments in southern Yorkshire and span at least the entire area from the River Don to the Calder Valley and probably beyond, although data is limited by previous research parameters (Sidebottom, 1994 and 2000). The Elmet Group attributes are as follows (Sidebottom, 1994):

1. An incised or grooved carving technique.
2. Plain areas which are otherwise undecorated, but carefully finished.
3. The use of a distinctive inner groove providing a framework to both decorated and plain areas.

However, in the wider Elmet region there are more tightly defined (in a geographical sense) specific attributes which indicate localized sub-groups within the larger regional repertoire. These have additional design elements to the iconographic 'package' found throughout the wider region, as outlined above. One 'sub-group' has been identified in the present Kirklees area to both the north and south of the River Calder, a discrete group that is found in the Pennine foothills in the Huddersfield–Batley region. It is recognized by the addition of particular scroll, interlace and animal art characteristics, in addition to the standard Elmet design elements. Geographically, this group occupies the steeper river valleys of West Yorkshire and relatively poorer soils, an area where there was likely to have been a large Hiberno-Norse input, and includes the Saxon-period estates in which the three more specifically 'Norse' monuments are located. These sites are at Birstall, Hartshead and Rastrick, as well as at Kirkheaton, with monuments also at the 'shared' (with another group – see below) site of Thornhill, not far from Dewsbury.

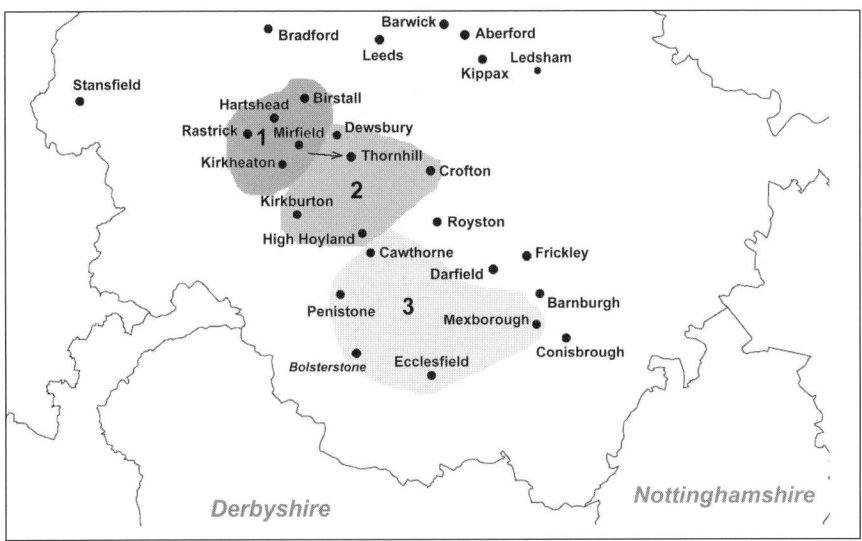

Fig. 39: Regional groups of monuments in south-west Yorkshire.

Another group is also located in the Calder Valley, but has a wider distribution and is largely found lower down the valley than the monuments of the 'Kirklees' group, at Thornhill, Dewsbury, Crofton, Kirkburton and as far south as High Hoyland, the latter on the border between West and South Yorkshire, to the north-west of Barnsley. The monuments at Thornhill are extensive and share design elements with the 'Kirklees' group, suggesting that it may have been the centre of an estate which included the upper reaches of the Calder Valley, later to become fragmented, creating smaller estates in their own right, but still having some form of authority over them. The inscriptions suggest some degree of literacy here. Much the same arrangement appears to have transpired on the Wirral, where several surviving monument sites on the boggy land that was reclaimed by the Hiberno-Norse in the tenth century are reflected in the array of monument fragments now on display at the church of St John, Chester, which was undoubtedly the mother church to the old estate, which included the Wirral to its north-west (see Bailey, 1980).

In South Yorkshire, there is an additional group within the greater Elmet array of sculpted stones. The signature attributes of this group are quite interesting and, like the other groups described here, define a geographic region. The sites are at Cawthorne, Penistone, Ecclesfield and Mexborough. There is also a fragment of a cross shaft built into the porch wall at Conisbrough which appears to be from the Elmet group of monuments, but it is too fragmentary to say more. Other stone cross shafts in South Yorkshire have, at one time, been described as 'pre-Conquest' – at Barnburgh, Rawmarsh and Thrybergh – but are almost certainly post-Conquest in date (Ryder, 1982; Sidebottom, 1994 and 1997; Coatsworth, 2008). A carved stone, often thought to be Anglo-Saxon, which is built into the church wall at Sprotbrough (Coatsworth, 2008, p.251) may be a reused Roman decorative frieze.

All monuments of the group are incised and have some areas of plain, finely dressed stone which are otherwise undecorated. The significant motifs are a series of incised, often abstract symbols which appear meaningless to us. To the north, the Calder Valley group is similar, but the incised motifs are replaced by a stylized scroll design; the cut of the monuments is more 'grooved' than incised, and in general the execution of the carvings is more 'elegant', at least to our eyes. In many ways, they are more easily recognized as Anglo-Saxon when compared with their South Yorkshire counterparts. The incised motifs at Ecclesfield and elsewhere were even recognized as part of a distinct group by Collingwood in the earlier part of the twentieth century. He termed it the 'D-motif' group due to the reoccurrence of a symbol resembling several 'Ds', either in a rectangle (at Penistone and Cawthorne) or a circle as at Ecclesfield (Collingwood, 1927, pp.178–79). To this corpus of monuments may be added a slightly different circular incised motif at Mexborough, which also appears to be part of the same group, having small 'D-shapes' within the circles (Sidebottom, 1994 and 1997).

The similarity between the South Yorkshire cross shafts suggests a notion of shared cultural identity, real or manufactured. Like other groups of monuments in midland England, they project an expression of group cohesiveness (Sidebottom, 2000 and 2020). Although erected during the Anglo-Scandinavian settlement period, the monuments do not show any stylistic elements normally associated with Anglo-Scandinavian art, simply because they were not erected in areas of primary Scandinavian settlement. It is likely that a large amount of control over the estates of this region remained 'native', even though they probably paid tribute to Anglo-Saxon and (later) Anglo-Scandinavian overlords in the Vale of York. The integrity of the group of monuments suggests that a small unit existed within southern Elmet (if that is what it was), north of the River Don, that felt some sort of detachment from other Elmetian groups, even though this difference may have been of minor significance. The identity of the group, of course, remains unknown; interestingly, the very distinctive Barnsley accent developed in this area.

The cross base at Ecclesfield has two socket-holes, which are not unusual for Saxon-period monuments. Similar examples can be found in eastern Cheshire at Lyme Handley (the 'Bow Stones'), Disley churchyard and Ludworth ('Robin Hood's Pickling Rods'), and of course at Bolsterstone in South Yorkshire. The base and cross shaft at Ecclesfield are almost certainly contemporary, since the same form of decoration and carving technique is present on both and the surviving shaft fits well into the socket hole. At the time of writing, another possible cross shaft has been discovered in the churchyard, but has yet to be fully recorded. Why two cross shafts were erected together in the same base is uncertain, but they may have signified joint ownership of a land unit, a close (possibly family) affinity between two individuals or kin groups stating their authority in the political landscape.

It is not possible to find even a similar iconographic parallel elsewhere in England. Instead, the decorative elements displayed on this South Yorkshire group of stones are very similar to monuments found on the western seaboard in Wales and in Galloway in south-west Scotland. The pre-Conquest stone monuments of Wales show, essentially, two different styles. Some of them, particularly those around coastal areas, are similar to the Anglo-Scandinavian monuments of the Isle of Man and Cumbria. They are highly decorated crosses with plaits and interlaces usually associated with Anglo-Scandinavian art. It seems reasonable to assume that these were the monuments erected by the Norse during their settlement of these regions. The other style of monument in Wales is similar to those found in other so-called 'Celtic' areas of Britain and in Brittany. These are incised slabs and monoliths, sometimes with Latin or Ogham inscriptions, and have incised carving; they are similar to the cross shaft at Ecclesfield and the other sculptures of the South Yorkshire group. Fig. 40 shows the Ecclesfield cross and that at Cawthorne compared with stones at Ardwall Isle in Galloway and at Nevern in Wales. Note how Collingwood's 'D-pattern' can be seen on all of the stones. In addition, all of these monuments contain large areas of undecorated dressed stonework and are inscribed rather than carved in relief, unlike almost all other English pre-Conquest freestanding sculpture.

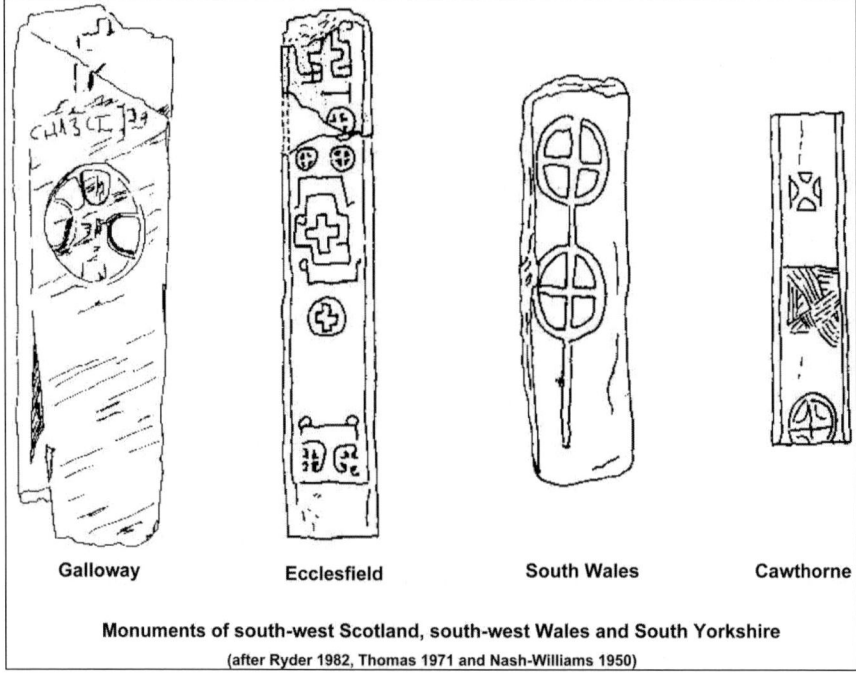

Galloway   Ecclesfield   South Wales   Cawthorne

Monuments of south-west Scotland, south-west Wales and South Yorkshire
(after Ryder 1982, Thomas 1971 and Nash-Williams 1950)

Fig. 40: South Yorkshire and British crosses.

Around the turn of the last century, the inscribed stones in Wales (and elsewhere) were dated, again, as a chronological stylistic sequence from as early as the fifth century onwards. However, the main criteria for such dates are the stylistic evolution of text – epigraphic development (see Nash-Williams, 1950) – as well as decorative evolution. More recently, the dating of the 'Celtic' stones has also received critical attention; 'art history, epigraphy and historical associations do not ... enable us to construct a detailed chronology for these monuments' (Dark, 1992, p.60). Dark's paper states that some of the so-called 'early' inscribed stones cannot be dated with any accuracy and may even be contemporary with the highly-decorated monuments in England. In similar vein, Smyth (1979, p.290) concludes that almost all pre-Conquest carved stone monuments in Ireland may be from the tenth century rather than forming a chronological series over several centuries.

Of the British place-name elements in southern Yorkshire, discussed above, those of the 'brettas' group are of interest to the carved stones in South Yorkshire. Taylor (1992, p.124) notes that five such names occur in the old West Riding; two between the Calder and Aire and three close to the headwaters of the Don and its tributaries. The northern pair of Bretta names – Burton Salmon and Birkby Hill – are far less convincing than those around the Don watershed – Monk Bretton, West Bretton and Britland Edge. Fig. 41 shows the locations of these place-names and it can be seen that they enclose the northern and eastern limits of the group of inscribed monuments. The series of 'in-Elmet' place-names to the north appear to delineate the boundary of the ancient kingdom (Faull and Moorhouse, 1981, pp.171–72), and this seems to be reflected through the iconography of the monuments on each side of the boundary. In the case of the three 'brettas' place-names, they may have held the same function. Given the cohesiveness of their geographical distribution and their distinctive iconography, this particular group of southern Yorkshire monuments suggests that they identify a small, otherwise unknown

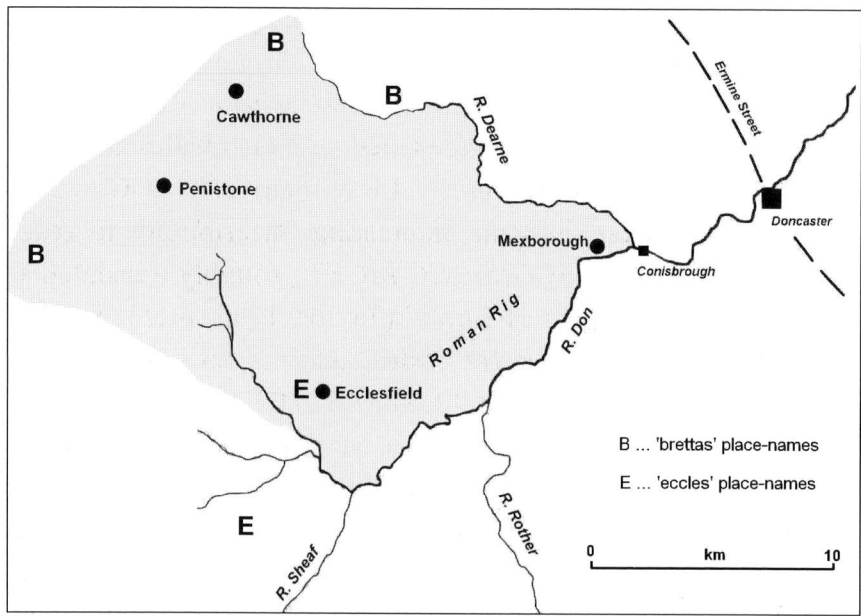

Fig. 41: Cross shafts with British names.

unit within the wider Elmet landscape that was particularly 'British' in character.

Along with the 'brettas' place-names in this area are two 'eccles' place-name elements that survive today (Ecclesfield and Ecclesall). It was suggested above that they may be linked to Hiberno-Norse settlers in distinctively British regions during the tenth century, where their presence buttressed the continuing use of British name-elements and adds further evidence for a fundamentally British character to the district. It is probable that this area comprised a single multiple estate which was, eventually, fragmented into component parts, Hallamshire (or its predecessor in name – discussed later) being one of these. As mentioned earlier, these large estates were originally almost akin to small kingdoms, as indeed has been suggested for *Loidis*, as described above. It is notable that the monuments are all to the north of the River Don, and interestingly, the land unit that they describe also contains the Roman Rig earthworks along its south-eastern flank. It has geographic integrity, being bounded by the River

Don, the River Dearne and the higher Pennine ground to the north-west.

It has already been discussed that some form of 'ethnic' or dynastic ties existed between the rulers of North Wales and those of Elmet. A carved stone on the Lleyn Peninsula in Gwynedd (north-west Wales) has an interesting inscription; it reads '*ALIORTUS ELMETIACO(S) HIC IACET*', roughly translated as 'here lies Aliortus, man of Elmet' (Taylor, 1992, p.111; Breeze, 2002, p.160). The stone (or rather its inscription) has been stylistically dated to *c*. AD 500 (Breeze, 2002, p.160), but note previous comments concerning the unreliability of such dating methods, so this could well be later. Fig. 40 shows the similarity of design to sculpted stones in west Wales, so the obvious conclusion seems to be that in South Yorkshire – at least between the upper Don and Dearne valleys – there was a small group that thought of themselves as British, with little or no affinity to the Anglo-Saxons; it is tempting to see Aliortus as a man perhaps from what would become Barnsley in South Yorkshire. It is clear that many of the small groups known to us from the *Tribal Hidage* and other sources continued to exist beyond the Viking settlement of the ninth and tenth centuries (Sidebottom, 2020), and such is suggested here for the inhabitants of at least this part of southern Elmet: a small group paying tribute perhaps, initially, to the rulers of Elmet, who in turn paid for their semi-independence to the greater lords of the richer lands to the east. It was a land unit that was probably little known to the outside world and disappeared without trace before it made it into 'history'. This cultural identity displayed in the earlier part of the tenth century, as argued here, would have soon disintegrated following the Anglo-Saxon reorganization of the political landscape in the second half of the tenth century.

The fragmentation of the old large estates, the imposition of 'foreign' landowners, the changing economic focus through the growth of towns and the effects of unification combined to destroy regional identity. However, ethnicity is not only an emotive word, it is a term frequently misunderstood and is often confused with racial origins; the two are different. In the case of this mysterious people group (if it ever really existed), group cohesiveness is more likely to have been sustained by a sense of common purpose than anything else. Local identity meant farming the same type of landscape, sharing the same topographical problems and, possibly, feeling a sense of being somewhat marginalized yet perhaps at the same time being pioneers. Any notion of racial identity was likely to have been secondary or even non-existent until times of stress. When faced with the likelihood of major changes and possible losses following the West Saxon takeover of Viking-controlled land during the tenth century, such a time existed. Proud origins, however much diluted, were resurrected and displayed in stone to demonstrate this group identity.

To the east of the Ecclesfield group are a small number of cross fragments at Conisbrough, Frickley, Roystone and Barnburgh. They are separated from the Ecclesfield group by the River Dearne and, in the case of Roystone, are located on small tributary feeds into it. Their locations form a ribbon of sites extending north by north-west from Conisbrough, all west of the Magnesian Limestone ridge and Ermine Street; interestingly, the latter is a part of South Yorkshire where there are no monument sites. The Barnburgh fragment is a small part of a cross head and it is difficult to identify it to a regional group due to a lack of iconographic diagnostic elements; the cut (in a raised-relief carving technique which is often termed 'moulded'), however, is very different from the Ecclesfield group, which has an incised carving technique. Frickley, Conisbrough and Roystone do have iconographic similarities between them; the carving technique, like the Barnburgh fragment, is moulded on all of the shafts, while they display common interlace types and have a very distinctive spiral edge moulding. Unlike the Ecclesfield group, the monuments are more traditionally 'Anglo-Saxon' in their design.

Fig. 42: Monuments of the Frickley group (from Coatsworth 2008, reproduced by courtesy of the Corpus of Anglo-Saxon Stone Sculpture).

Whether the Frickley, Conisbrough, Barnburgh and Roystone monument fragments together form a discrete regional group in their own right is uncertain, but they do appear to differ from monuments further to the north. For example, the two fragments at Crofton, now in West Yorkshire, some 6km north-east of Royston, have different design elements and have been identified to the Calder Valley group (Sidebottom, 1994). What this may represent is evidence for two distinct groups in South Yorkshire north of the River Don. One was essentially a British people-group north of the upper reaches of the Don Valley and east of the Dearne, the other an Anglo Scandinavian encroachment westwards from the Ermine Street corridor. The latter encroachment included the key strategic sites of Conisbrough and Barnburgh, along with the Ryknield Street crossing of the Don at Strafford Sands.

Fig. 43: Monuments of the Ecclesfield group (from Coatsworth 2008, reproduced by courtesy of the Corpus of Anglo-Saxon Stone Sculpture).

The missing monuments

The distribution of freestanding stone monuments in general corresponds to that of estate centres, and as such they are, in most areas, dispersed in a fairly uniform pattern across the landscape. In areas of high agricultural yield, for example in the Vale of York, they are relatively close together, while in areas with poorer soils they are somewhat further apart where there seems to have been a slower process of fragmentation of the old estates. This is clearly demonstrated in the distribution of monuments in the Peak District, most of southern Yorkshire, Lincolnshire and the north Midlands, but there is a large area between them which is entirely devoid of freestanding monuments. Whilst it is true that in some areas their lack of survival into modern times has inevitably led to 'holes' in the pattern of distribution, this is unlikely to explain why such a large

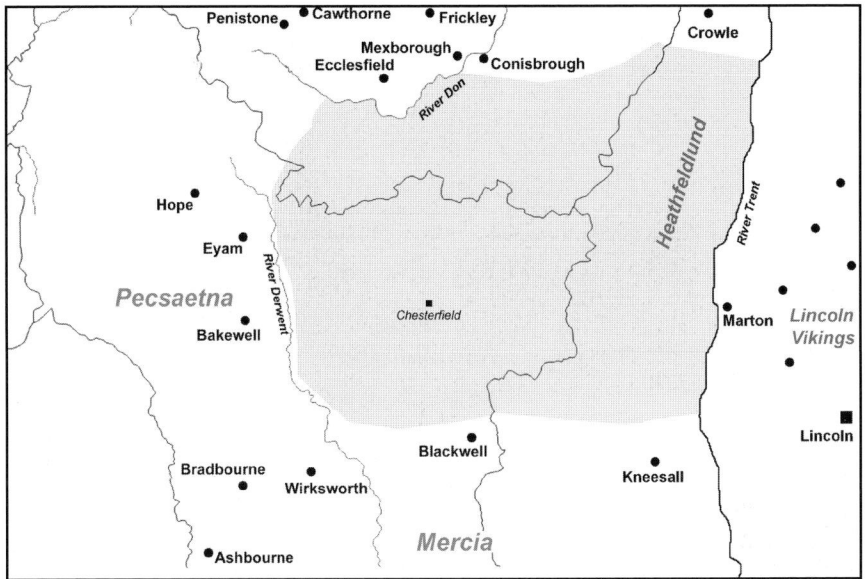

Fig. 44: The monument void.

area has no monuments at all. This void stretches from the River Don in South Yorkshire southwards across present-day north-east Derbyshire and north Nottinghamshire, as far as Blackwell, near Alfreton, in Derbyshire and Kneesall in Nottinghamshire. In the west, monuments in the Peak District are curtailed close to the River Derwent, with no further examples in an easterly direction as far as the eastern side of the River Trent (data from Sidebottom, 1994; Everson and Stocker, 1999 and 2016; Coatsworth, 2008; and Hawkes and Sidebottom, 2018).

All of the extant monuments around this region that are not too fragmentary fall into distinct and separate regional groups. Those in the Peak District and north-eastern Derbyshire are either monuments of a Peak District group or a Trent Valley (Mercian) group (Sidebottom, 2020), those in Lincolnshire and at Kneesall in Nottinghamshire are monuments of the Lincoln Vikings (Sidebottom, 1994 and 2000) and those in South Yorkshire, north of the Don in Elmet, are discussed above. The area south of the River Don is, therefore, one that lies between political groupings, leading to questions over why this area shows no monumental evidence and, by inference, no administrative estate centres. The most likely answer has already been alluded to earlier in this discussion, being related to the fact that the frontier between Northumbria and Mercia, before the Viking settlement, was always contentious. The earthworks and place-names to the immediate north of the River Don suggest that the frontier between the kingdoms was here (at least for a while), while south of the river there was no stability of tenure and the area thus held the potential to become a war zone at any time. Battles were fought along Ermine Street, between Littleborough in north Nottinghamshire and Doncaster. There were no significant geographical features in what became southern South Yorkshire and north-east Derbyshire to enable some form of natural separation between one area and another, so it was difficult – to say the least – to create a defendable line of demarcation within it.

This was not an area of rich agricultural land, being notable for its woodland regeneration after the collapse of the Roman economy. It could thus be all but abandoned for the sake of easing political tensions between the two kingdoms. The archaeological evidence for Anglo-Saxon settlement, or rather lack of it, until towards the very end of the period also lends support to this hypothesis. However, it is discussed above that the Viking settlement changed the political dynamics of this region, removing the potential for warfare that had existed beforehand, but this was a process which had barely begun when the freestanding crosses were being erected.

What we see through study of the monuments is a snapshot of the politics in this region by the first half of the tenth century. By then, what became north-east Derbyshire was under the jurisdiction of the Mercian Vikings, as far as we know, but settlement expansion into this area of regenerated woodland and heath does not appear to have extended further northwards than Blackwell, near Alfreton. The monument at the church there displays the same design elements as cross shafts found in Derby at the church of St Alkmund (Hawkes and Sidebottom, 2018, pp.145–46). Blackwell church is located less than 4km to the east of the Roman road, Ryknield Street, which linked Derby to Templeborough in South Yorkshire, and stands on a hilltop, well away from the present village. The church is dedicated to St Werburgh, another Mercian dedication (along with Alkmund), which Stafford (1985) suggests may have been fostered during the early to mid-tenth century, as Anglo-Saxon Mercian identity appeared threatened by the growing power of the West Saxons. The church's unusually prominent location is interesting; it is built on the eastern side of a knoll which rises from an escarpment edge, elevating the building even further above the surrounding landscape. The western side of the knoll appears as a contoured earthwork (see Fig. 47) which is now cut by the steeply climbing road passing by the church, although it appears to continue around the western edge of the churchyard, itself unusually large and irregular. It is tempting to see this rather unusual topography as not entirely natural and possibly the reuse of a much earlier site (Sidebottom, 2008, pp.77–81). Such a prominent location suggests that it was more of a strategic site than anything else, with an eye on Ryknield Street, clearly visible to the north-west.

At the northern end of Ryknield Street was the old Roman fort at Templeborough, where the Roman Rig earthworks protected the north bank of the River Don and its crossing at Strafford Sands, close to Conisbrough. The river crossing could be better monitored here after the shifting of the axis of control away from Doncaster and towards the important centre at Conisbrough, where archaeological evidence for an Anglo-Saxon and Viking presence is manifest. Of interest to this discussion is Chesterfield, the site of a former Roman fort located well into the zone between the River Don and the Mercian centre at Blackwell. Chesterfield is a rare former Roman centre that not only was abandoned after the collapse of the Roman economy, but also, unlike Derby or Doncaster, appears to practically disappear in the pre-Conquest period, to the extent that it appears only as one of six berewicks of Newbold by 1086 (Williams and Martin, 1992, p.741). The old Ryknield Street Roman road also shows that it was abandoned as a routeway during the Anglo-Saxon period. Roman roads survived

Fig. 45: Distant view of Blackwell church and earthworks.

Fig. 46: Blackwell vista – Ryknield Street is in the distance.

Fig. 47: Blackwell escarpment.

far better when they were kept in use, good local examples being Ermine Street north of Doncaster, Till Bridge Lane between Lincoln and Littleborough on the River Trent, and King's Street through the limestone Peak District. There are many similar examples throughout England where former Roman roads were useful to the Anglo-Saxon and Viking-period leaders to mobilize armies quickly over distances. In the case of Roman Ryknield Street, its course can be traced from Derby as far as Stretton in north-east Derbyshire, close to Blackwell. But further north, and certainly in what became South Yorkshire, the road became untraceable as a Roman highway, suggesting that it was abandoned as a military route after the Roman period.

So it would seem that north-east Derbyshire (as it became) and South Yorkshire, south of the Don, was an area of abandonment by the beginning of the tenth century. Similar comments apply to *Heathfelthlund* between the rivers Idle and Trent, where no monuments are found and the line of the old Roman road between

Scaftworth and Doncaster became untraceable. The only stone cross in this area is found at Crowle, at the head of the Humber estuary, on the Isle of Axholme. Interestingly, Crowle stands on the same 'island' in the fens where evidence has been found for a Roman-period island site at Trent Falls, which might have acted as a transhipment port for agricultural goods from the Humberhead Levels (Van de Noort, 2003, p.260), and it is possible that Crowle was its early-medieval successor. The Crowle cross shaft is said to be Northumbrian in style (Everson and Stocker, 2016, pp.147–50), in that it broadly fits with monuments of the York Vikings, rather than the Lincoln Vikings, and indeed the stone type is likely to be reused material from Roman York. There is a fragmentary inscription which again refers to a 'beacon' and follows the usual successive formula of erected by 'x', after 'y' (ibid.). There are two possibilities: either the shaft was erected to mark the authority of the York Vikings in what had remained, or developed as, an administrative centre at the Humber's head, or it was brought to Crowle at a later date as a curio. Indeed, it was not recorded at Crowle before the nineteenth century (Everson and Stocker, 2016, p.147).

By 942, therefore, there was a line of demarcation in the landscape which separated Yorkshire (the jurisdiction of the northern kingdom based on York) from the north Midlands, now subsumed into a conquered Mercia and under West Saxon control (Garmonsway, 1953, pp.60, 110). This relatively new border was to become long-lived and survived as the later Yorkshire–Derbyshire boundary until minor alterations occurred in the twentieth century. It was to the advantage of the West Saxons to keep this particular line as the border, since it was not a defendable demarcation and could be easily overcome, should the need arise, in the process of their conquest of the North. It was most likely the submission of the Vikings (and other groups) to the West Saxons in the first half of the tenth century that led to the greater stability in the area that for centuries had been denied.

Chapter 11

Later Saxon Estates in South Yorkshire

Changes in the countryside

After the fall of the Roman economy and its market system, the focus was on subsistence, and essentially anything that was needed was produced and consumed locally. The need for pottery diminished; once it had been a product of the market system (as it is today), fired in commercial kilns and distributed over a wide area. During the Roman period, pottery was even imported from abroad, especially via the military through their frequent trips to and from the European continent. But after the collapse of that market system, pottery was made locally, fired on bonfires as it had been before the Roman occupation, and in many cases probably substituted by vessels made from wood, hide and so on. Tools, again, would be made on a local scale, with greater reliance placed on consumables suited to the specific topography and geology of the local area. For example, arable agriculture would be more the focus of production on the rich lowland plains than on the hillslopes, where animal rearing would have predominated.

Administration, too, was focussed on various and diverse ecozones, with landholdings extending over relatively large areas. This was the origin of the so-called 'multiple estate', where a large enough land area would provide most of what was needed for consumption by those within it. In the land unit of the *Pecsaetna*, to the south-west of South Yorkshire, David Roffe's contention (1986) is that it was once a single large multiple estate based on an administrative centre at Bakewell. That estate centre would not have been a town or village as it is today, but more like a large farmstead with perhaps a hall and facilities for storage of commodities produced locally. Settlement was dispersed within the landscape, with small farms dotted about the countryside rather than the populace huddled together in houses within a village. Each small farmstead would have farmed the immediate landscape as a small component part of the larger estate. In some more peripheral areas, especially in northern England, settlement was previously less Romanized than in areas to the south, so economic change was less dramatic following the collapse of the Roman market economy, but there was still less opportunity to exchange home-produced goods for exotic wares from elsewhere. This is not to say that some form of market trading did not occur; it most likely did, but the basis of the post-Roman domestic economy was subsistence.

During the mid-Saxon period, the settlement pattern changed, in some areas this happened quite dramatically. Dispersed farmsteads were abandoned in favour of nucleated settlements; the familiar 'English village' now dominated the landscape. Rows of houses were clustered together along a roadway, with garden plots behind them, all set within a sea of open fields around the village. This is still a familiar sight in the present-day countryside. At the heart of the village was the hall – the residence of the lord of the manor – with the parish church nearby. Estates became smaller due to a process known as fragmentation, where the old multiple estates were gradually divided into smaller units until they became what we know from the late Saxon period as a manor. The reason for nucleation is not documented, but it is likely that it was to make the smaller estates – the new manors – more efficient by creating large tracts of open fields, with houses swept from the landscape and crammed together under the watchful eye of the new lord in his hall and, of course, the Church. Nucleation meant that the peasant farmer became disenfranchised and lost the means to subsist, becoming subject to the dictation of the lord of the manor and his agents. This was the true beginning of the medieval age and serfdom.

Accelerated fragmentation also followed warfare and conquest, with land given as a reward for military and political service. This is seen clearly in the gifting of estates following the Viking submission of the North to the West Saxons, where new landholdings were not only created to reward service, but also to dilute the power of existing landholders. The same thing happened after the Norman Conquest. Some of these new estates were given by charter, as discussed below. Nucleation began to occur in the south perhaps from around the late-eighth century, but this was not uniform across the country. In some areas – and the southern Pennines was probably one of them – nucleation followed much later, but by the time of the Norman Conquest most areas had succumbed; even then, especially in some upland areas, nucleation never occurred at all.

The charters

One form of evidence that can shed light on the development of landholdings is that gained from charters. However, there were far fewer charters in most areas of northern England than in the south. This is not to say that there were fewer land transactions; it is more a reflection on how land was ceded. In southern areas, one of the main forms of land transaction was through what was known as bookland. These were written charters that were usually held by the Church and provided a legal depository to the secular administration, another case of Church and state working in tandem, which was particularly favoured by the West Saxons (Loyn, 1984, pp.82, 89). In northern areas, most land transactions were made by traditional folkland ceremonics, often transacted at outdoor meeting places – 'moots' and 'things' – where the details of land cession were held as 'folk memory' and were never written down. Today, of course, this presents a significant drawback to our understanding of the formation of northern estates during the Anglo-Saxon and Anglo-Scandinavian periods.

We have already mentioned that Doncaster seems to have been a major centre – at least in a strategic sense – during the sixth and seventh centuries, possibly even continuing later than that. At some point it seems that Conisbrough also became an important centre, shifting the focus away from Doncaster, but this, according to Parker (1987, p.42), may have not been until the tenth century. Hadley (1996, p.6) adds that any notion of a considerable antiquity for the soke (large estate) of Conisbrough can be brought into question when we look closely at the evidence. We can agree with Hey that, at some point, the most important pre-Conquest *burh* in South Yorkshire became Conisbrough (a place-name meaning the 'king's stronghold'). However, as the name was not recorded until *c.* 1002, we have little idea when it first became a significant centre. The first part of the name, *'konungar'* (king), could be Old Norse, which would suggest that it was a Viking creation, although Hey (2003, p.27) points out that it might also refer to the earlier Anglo-Saxon word, *'cyning'*. During the medieval period, the church at Conisbrough was the minster to a comparatively large area, with many dependent chapelries (ibid., p.46), again indicating that Conisbrough had its roots as an early centre. But what is 'early'?

Documentary evidence before the *Domesday* account of 1086 is exceptionally rare in South Yorkshire, but we do have a small number of charters, almost all from the will of Wulfric Spott and dated to 1002–1004. Wulfric was part of the Anglo-Saxon aristocracy and was particularly favoured by the West Saxon ruling elite. His mother, Wulfrun, was the founder of the nunnery at Wolverhampton, and Wulfric himself founded Burton Abbey in Staffordshire (Smyth, 1987, p.91), which became the repository to the surviving documents referred to here. Fig. 48 shows the distribution of charters in South Yorkshire and north-east Derbyshire, of which all except one are from the will of Wulfric Spott. The exception is a charter (again from the collection at Burton Abbey) for land at Chesterfield dated 955, which was ceded to Uhtred, another West Saxon prodigy, whose kin held most or all of the former land unit of the *Pecsaetna*, a few kilometres to the west (Sidebottom, 2020, pp.111–18). This acquisition was probably strategic, to secure control of a former Roman fortified site following the West Saxon dominance of the North.

Wulfric's charter land comprised a large but compact cluster of landholdings in former Scandinavian-controlled areas (Sawyer, 1975, p.29) in what became South Yorkshire and north-east Derbyshire. The primary reason for this was to dilute local control in the region by the imposition of a landlord faithful to the West Saxon kings, but it is also probable that this was land in an area which was so far undeveloped and ripe for exploitation. We have already mentioned that the Coal Measures region of north-east Derbyshire seems to have been an area of extensive regenerated woodlands following the collapse of the Roman economy (see Rackham, 1986, pp.75–83). In addition, there are numerous place-name elements which refer to woodland; Elmton and Ashover are prime examples. Others suggest neglected agricultural land, such as Heath, Clay Lane and Brackenfield (Fellows-Jensen, 1978, p.257). In Yorkshire south of the Don, there are names such as Woodhouse, Woodthorpe or Fulwood, while the place-name *Wlvathuait* (later Woolthwaite) near Tickhill is said to mean a small clearing 'infested by wolves' (Smith, 1961, p.55), which perhaps says it all.

We do not know when these landholdings were created, because the charters only date to when they were ceded in 1002–1004 in Wulfric's will (Sawyer, 1975, p.30); they could have been well established by then, or they could be new holdings created at the time or just before, which is what is suggested here. It is recalled that all of the '…thorpe' names south of the River Don in South Yorkshire post-date the *Domesday* survey (Williams and Martin, 1992). It can be seen from Fig. 48 that the chartered estates form a swathe of relatively concentrated holdings from north of Blackwell, now in Derbyshire, as far as the borderlands with the Northumbrian kingdom based on York. These are all on the Coal Measures soils and are separated from the *Pecsaetna* lands to the west by the gritstone fringes of the Peak District. Further north, there are no charter lands between Beighton (now on the outskirts of Sheffield) and Conisbrough on the River Don, and this seems to be because the large estate based on Conisbrough extended to include most, or all, of this area (Sawyer, 1975, p.38), as discussed below.

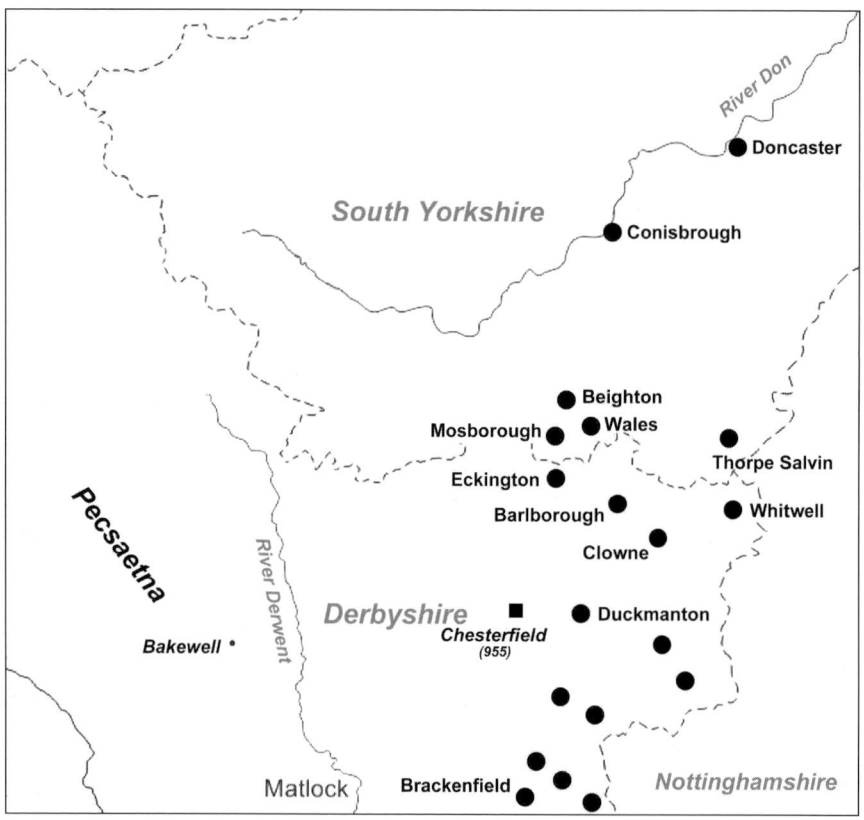

Fig. 48: Wulfric Spott's charters.

In the North, the old 'multiple estates', the large landholdings that characterized the early Saxon division of land tended to survive longer than their southern counterparts, which were perhaps closer in size to the late Saxon manorial holdings of the *Domesday* account (see Hadley, 1996, p.5). This particularly manifested itself in South Yorkshire, where the estate or soke of Conisbrough developed into an exceedingly large estate when compared with the landholdings in present-day north-east Derbyshire that were ceded in the will of Wulfric Spott. It is probably no coincidence that Conisbrough was under the control of the York Vikings until their authority became diminished during the tenth century, whereas those further south, in northern Mercia, were not. The 'new' frontier, which was described in 942, is plain to see in the charter landscape at the beginning of the eleventh century.

Some of the large estates of the North appear to predate the Viking settlement, although others show little sign of antiquity, and this includes the estate at Conisbrough, which Hadley (1996, p.6) sees as relatively late in formation and only developed after the importance of Doncaster had well and truly waned. It is argued above that Doncaster only lost its prominence after the new Viking-period border was formed between Dore and Whitwell, and especially after the submission of the North to the West Saxons. Parker and Hey note that there are indications that Doncaster was a town by the tenth century (Hey, 2003, pp.44–45), but that its importance quickly waned (Parker, 1987, pp.33–35). However, the evidence – both historical and archaeological – is slight and it could well be that a *burh* here simply referred to little more than a fortified strategic location, although the pottery recovered from various sites suggests it was an urban centre (see earlier discussion). Urban or not, by the beginning of the eleventh century, Doncaster was not the principal focus in southern Yorkshire; that was now Conisbrough, some 7km upstream on the River Don. Doncaster is included in the raft of charters from the will of Wulfric Spott, the only other known charter from South Yorkshire besides Conisbrough, but the status of Doncaster in *c.* 1002 is ambiguous. Hey (2003, pp. 44–45) notes that it is unclear whether Doncaster was independent from Conisbrough or a part of it, and little more than half a century later, the *Domesday* survey only includes Doncaster along with Warmsworth as a part of a larger estate based on Hexthorpe (Williams and Martin, 1992, p.809).

When Conisbrough became the dominant estate in southern Yorkshire (Hey, 2003, pp.44–45), it seems that its jurisdiction, during the later-tenth century and up to the beginning of the eleventh, extended right across South Yorkshire south of the River Don, as far as the Dore–Whitwell boundary. The focus of the 'stronghold' in Conisbrough itself is unknown; it may have been where the Norman castle is now, or on the bluff of land on which the church stands a few metres away. Hey (2003, p.45) suggests that the latter may have been the location of the wapentake meeting place. With Conisbrough established as the principal centre, from the late-tenth century onwards the southern Yorkshire political landscape changed dramatically. At some point, a second estate was formed within the Conisbrough soke centred on Laughton-en-le-Morthen, separated from Conisbrough by Ryknield Street and which may have been the otherwise unidentified Wulfric charter site of *Morlingtune* (ibid.). The name 'Morthyng' may well include the Scandinavian element 'thing' (Stein, 2019, p.6), which of course also suggests an origin in the Scandinavian period. Whatever the origins of Morthen, it seems likely that the estate – the 'Laughton' soke – came into existence during the early-eleventh century, or at the very end of the tenth as part of the rapid 'opening up' of South Yorkshire, south of the Don. It is probable that there was already some settlement in the area, but probably not long before; Cumberpatch notes the discovery of two Torksey-type ware rims dating to the period between the late-ninth and mid-eleventh centuries, and two sherds of Lincoln Kiln-type and Lincoln Shelly ware, both of late-ninth to late-tenth century date. It also produced the largest assemblage of Lincolnshire Fine-Shelled ware outside Lincolnshire, but this type was not in use until after the late-tenth century (Cumberpatch, 2016) and suggests that the focus of Laughton as a centre was indeed quite late in the Saxon period. Further eleventh-century development in this area is evidenced by a hoard of thirty-two, eleventh-century, Anglo-Saxon and Norman coins found in 1939 at Whiston, near Rotherham (SMR 00190/01).

Another developing centre in South Yorkshire was that of Tickhill with its former motte-and-bailey Norman castle, a settlement that developed, quickly, from the twelfth century onwards into a medieval town (Hey, 1979, p.50). At first glance, it would appear that this was the centre of an important and long-established landholding; however, the *Domesday* account shows that this was not so. Surprisingly, Tickhill itself is not mentioned in the *Domesday* survey; it was probably an unnamed hamlet within the estate of Dadsley, the

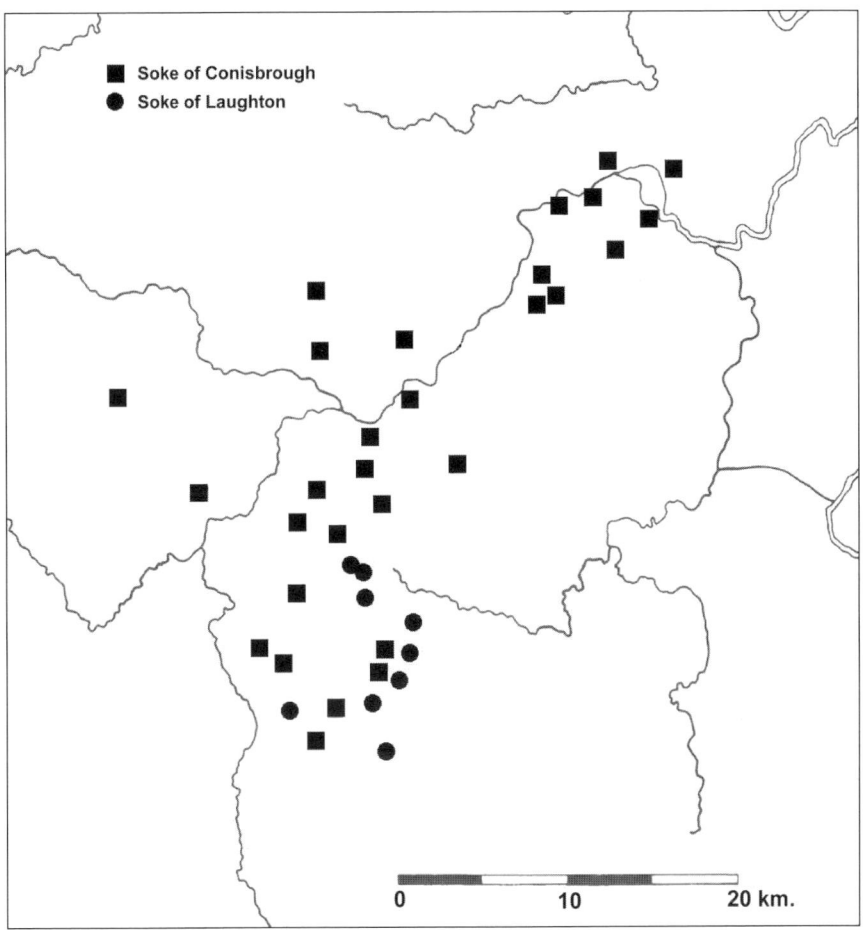

Fig. 49: The sokes of Conisbrough and Laughton.

latter almost certainly an eleventh-century fragmentation from the original Conisbrough estate (see Hey, 1979, p 30). The choice of Tickhill (Dadsley) as a Norman fortified site appears to have been strategic, just the same as the Viking-controlled settlements around Maltby and Hellaby, some 7km to the west, had been in the tenth century. The Viking settlements could control movement along Ryknield Street, but Tickhill could also turn its focus onto the Roman road crossing of the River Idle – formerly the borderland between southern Northumbria and *Heathfelthlund* – which was only 5 or 6km to the east.

The sequence of estate formation in South Yorkshire before the Norman Conquest is unknown, relying on little more than informed guesswork. The evidence from stone monuments, discussed earlier, suggests that some people-groups can be identified in Pennine Yorkshire north of the River Don, seemingly representing a small number of large estates. In South Yorkshire, the most indicative is that which stretches from Ecclesfield to Mexborough along the north bank of the River Don and northwards between the Dearne Valley and the upper Don watershed. The identity of this people-group – if that is what it represents – is unknown and seemingly does not survive as an identifiable unit following later reorganization of the political landscape as it presents itself through the *Domesday* survey. This is probably due to the fragmentation of estates and, in particular, the deliberate dispersal of large blocks of landholding by the West Saxon centralised control over the North, and indeed a similar breakdown of power-blocks was carried out by the Normans. In the case of the postulated Ecclesfield/Mexborough/Cawthorne/Penistone landholding, it became divided between two wapentakes and a number of different landowners. Besides this estate or people-group, as it probably once was, there seems to be some form of separate, but cohesive, estate on its eastern edge, east of the Dearne, north of Doncaster, but west of the upper reaches of the marshlands of the Humberhead Levels. It seems to have been focussed on Frickley and Roystone, with (most likely) Barnburgh being its centre. This landholding, as discussed above, was probably 'ethnically' different in that it may well have been under the control of, and possibly settled by, Anglo-Scandinavians who were able to protect the delicate Doncaster–Barnburgh frontier along the north–south Roman roads.

Perhaps most importantly, the negative evidence of where monuments are not found suggests that there were no centres of administration south of the River Don when they were erected. This is supported by the evidence from charters, which, as it is contended here, all concerned landholdings which post-dated the erection of the crosses in the first-half of the tenth century. Beyond this, we are reliant on the *Domesday* account which followed more than half a century after the charters were issued and more than a century after the crosses were erected. Many changes had been brought into effect in this rapidly developing landscape by the time *Domesday* was compiled.

Wapentakes and shires

Elsewhere in South Yorkshire, the composition of the wapentakes described in the *Domesday* survey of 1086 was likely to have been based largely on the multiple estates that preceded them, or an amalgamation of several of them in some cases. These were not necessarily of any great antiquity and may have reflected relatively late Anglo-Scandinavian period reorganization. The three *Domesday* wapentakes of South Yorkshire are Strafford, Staincross and a small part of Osgoldcross. Interestingly, Strafford wapentake, which includes all of the land south of the Don, is in two parts – 'Upper' and 'Lower' – relating to the topography (see Smith, 1961). The division of the two Strafford parts does, however, mirror the jurisdiction of Doncaster in the 'Lower' part and Conisbrough in the 'Upper'. The latter also includes some of the *Domesday* manors north of the River Don, between the River Dearne and the upper Don region around Ecclesfield, and incorporated much or all of the old Roman Rig earthworks. Conisbrough itself also stands just west of the division between the two parts of the wapentake, reflecting its early dominance over the wider area.

West of Conisbrough and south of the River Don is a relatively large area which now includes Rotherham and Sheffield and the 'shire' of Hallamshire. In the west of this area are the Millstone Grit uplands of the Pennines, which arguably were little used except perhaps for some seasonal grazing, but settlement was severely limited, even by the eleventh century. The exceptionally-large medieval manor and parish of Bradfield demonstrates this well, with vast tracts of moorland, steep valleys and odd patches of pasture controlled from a single centre. After the establishment of the Morthen estate by the early-eleventh century, the sequential development of land in South Yorkshire, south of the River Don, was likely to have been a fairly rapid westward encroachment, beginning with Rotherham as a principal centre, at the confluence of the rivers Don and Rother, and ending with the development of Hallamshire. South Yorkshire continued to be within the Danelaw, even beyond *Domesday*, and further Norse immigration is likely to have occurred, with settlers adept at making the most of upland landscapes. Most telling is the use of 'Bierlow' in the parishes of Brampton, Brightside and Ecclesall, a Norse word for a small administrative district (Institute for Name Studies, 2019).

Hallamshire was an area of South Yorkshire which seemingly included the settlements at Sheffield, Bradfield and Ecclesfield (Hey, 2002). However, its exact bounds are unknown, and it has an equally-obscure origin. These particular 'shires' are smaller land units within the larger counties, the latter promoted by the West Saxons to reorganize the political landscape, especially in the Midlands (Gelling, 1992, pp.141–42). In the Danelaw – especially in Yorkshire – 'shire' is a term that was also used for what would otherwise be termed a multiple estate, a large administrative area; other examples include Allertonshire, Richmondshire and Howdenshire. There has been an assumption that these were ancient units, but again the term 'ancient' is subjective because larger estates such as these did exist for longer in the northern Danelaw (see Hadley, 1996) and could have been formed at a relatively-late date.

In the case of Hallamshire, the name was not recorded until it was cited in a charter dated 1161 (Hey, 2002, p.9), most likely being a hybrid name containing the Norse element, '*hallr*' (Smith, 1961, p.194). There have been several attempts to reconstruct the boundary of Hallamshire. The general consensus is that Ecclesfield was its administrative centre (Hey, 2002) and it was a territory that seems to have only respected late-Saxon boundaries, including part of the

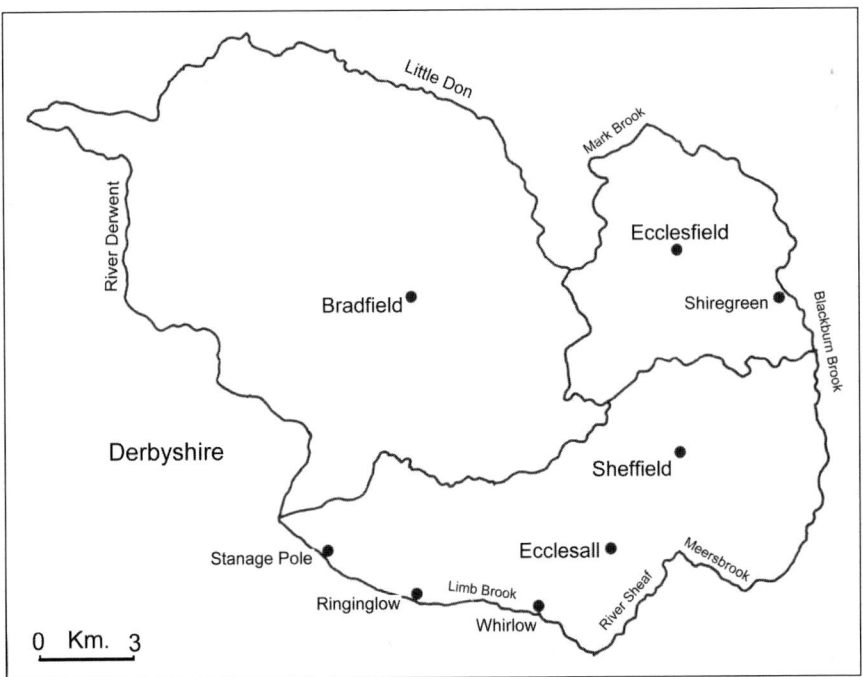

Fig. 50: Hallamshire (after Hey, 1979).

Dore–Whitwell demarcation. All indications suggest that Hallamshire was not formed until the latter stages of the 'opening-up' of the South Yorkshire landscape, south of the Don, and this may even have post-dated the Norman Conquest. It was that part of the Coal Measures – probably the last to be formed – that was administered from an existing centre, north of the River Don at Ecclesfield, and formed the western part of the Upper Strafforth wapentake. Fig. 51 shows the relationship of Hallamshire (after Hey, 1979 and 2002) in the context of stone monument distribution and later wapentakes. If this reconstruction is correct, Hallamshire can be seen to respect the late-Saxon manorial and wapentake boundaries of southern Yorkshire, but it does not respect the (arguably) earlier land unit described by the distribution of the South Yorkshire group of stone monuments (see Fig. 41). Again, this is an indication that Hallamshire was not an 'ancient' land unit.

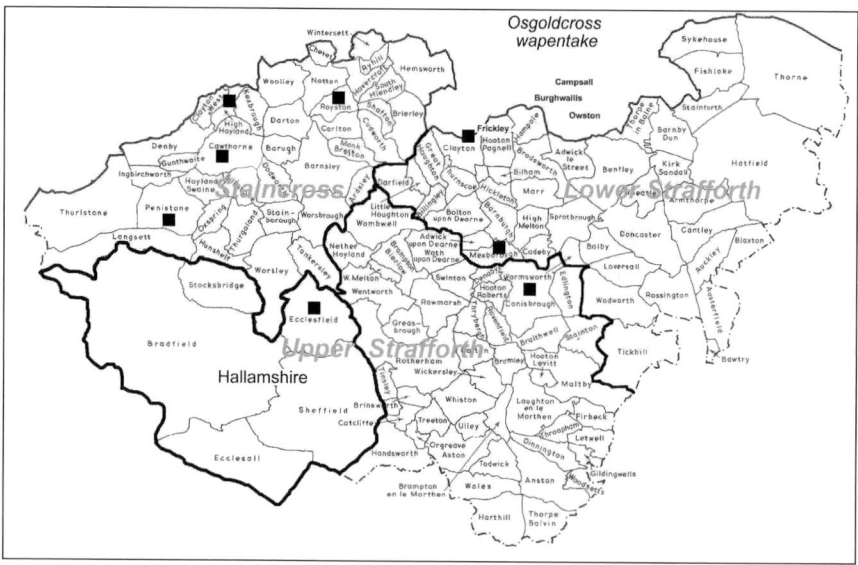

Fig. 51: Hallamshire and monument sites (based on Smith, 1961).

North of the River Don is the wapentake of Staincross (meaning stone cross), which arguably was once part of the old kingdom of Elmet behind the defences along the north bank of the Don. However, the old Rig earthworks were now contained largely in the newly-created Strafforth wapentake, and their separation from the main administrative centres of Staincross may well have been political and deliberate. Hey (2003, pp. 23–24) notes that the western end of the Roman Rig is irrelevant to the boundary of Hallamshire, again suggesting that Hallamshire was created long after the earthwork formed any kind of strategic boundary function. Staincross is now the name of a village to the north of Barnsley, but the wapentake bearing its name contained the old administrative centres of Royston, High Hoyland, Penistone and Cawthorne, which identify themselves through the stone monuments, dated here to the first half of the tenth century. Whilst Ecclesfield was once part of this group as another of its administrative centres, it became detached when the land to the south of the Don was developed and thereafter became the focus of Hallamshire wapentake. There also appears to have been a reorganization of the political landscape elsewhere north of the Don in Staincross wapentake. Hey (2003, p.48) suggests that Cawthorne, Dodworth, Hoylandswaine, Thurgoland, Barnsley and Stainborough (with detached parts at Cumberworth and West Bretton) were probably once part of an estate based on Stainborough/Silkstone, and that Darton, Penistone and High Hoyland were also part of this unit, although they seemingly became separate centres through the process of estate fragmentation and reorganization.

Lower Strafforth wapentake was largely focussed on the old centre at Doncaster and the potentially-strategic Roman road from Lincoln, but it also extended to include land formerly in the northern part of *Haethfeldlund*. The landscape here was in the marshlands of the lower Don and contained areas of slightly-elevated dry ground to the west of the Isle of Axholme. Settlements such as Fishlake or Stainforth on the lower Don are even now frequently prone to flooding, despite the efforts of the drainage engineer, Cornelius Vermuyden, who canalized and embanked many of the river courses in this area during the seventeenth century. The extension of settlement eastwards in this area can be seen as paralleling the encroachment into the Pennine foothills in the west of South Yorkshire. There was perhaps also a political dimension, and we are reminded that Gelling (1992, pp.141–42) argued that many boundaries in this region were essentially created from nothing by the West Saxons as a deliberate policy to destroy the cohesion of local groups. The division of *Heathfelthlund* bears the same hallmark, destroying any cohesive identity its inhabitants may have still held to this ancient land unit and diluting or destroying any notions of (in this case) topographical 'oneness'.

Most of Osgoldcross wapentake is within West Yorkshire, and includes Pontefract, Castleford and also Snaith, the latter now in East Yorkshire. Those few parishes that now find themselves in South Yorkshire comprise just Burghwallis, Campsall and Owston, arguably 'fen edge' settlements to the west of the present A19 and flanking the eastern side of Ermine Street. The evidence from tenth-century stone monuments suggests that this area was then regarded as politically separate from the rest of South Yorkshire, and this seems to have been reflected when the wapentakes in the old West Riding of Yorkshire were developed.

The boundary between Yorkshire and Derbyshire appears to have been more or less fixed by the mid-tenth century, continuing to follow the Dore–Whitwell line until the twentieth century. This demarcation remained politically sensitive as the fear of a resurrected kingdom based on York still lingered, even beyond the Norman Conquest, and maintaining territorial integrity here was important. However, the formation of shires in the north Midlands was relatively late. Neither Derbyshire nor Nottinghamshire were mentioned until the early eleventh century, and again appear to have been created from practically nothing by the West Saxons. The West Saxons were probably also responsible for the introduction of wapentakes and hundreds after their conquest of the various Viking groups of the Midlands. Their geographical areas are best known from the *Domesday* survey, although by then the parameters of many of them are likely to have been changed, as indeed they continued to be up to the thirteenth century (Gelling, 1992, p.142).

The formation of shires and wapentakes no doubt continued the process of fragmentation of power, just as the meting out of dispersed landholdings was after the Norman Conquest. With this in mind, it is difficult to assess the antiquity of many of the suspected relics of multiple estates, largely indicated by area place-names. Some might have been in existence for centuries by the time of the Norman Conquest, like the 'in-Elmet' or 'in-Craven' names further north appear to have been. Alternatively, some may have been created in response to the changing political divisions of the eleventh century. In the South Yorkshire region, Hey draws attention to Lindrick as a district name – now preserved in several place-names – which may have been one of those shadowy territories that formed sub-divisions of northern Mercia. Others include territories such as Ashfield (now in

Nottinghamshire), Balne or Morthen, the latter, as suggested above, having its origins in the eleventh century. Some of the district names may have been areas of forest, especially in the case of those on the reforested Magnesian Limestone belt around north Nottinghamshire (Hey, 2000, p.41).

Chapter 12

The Anglo-Saxon Church in South Yorkshire

One of the most obvious survivals of the pre-Conquest period is the number of church buildings that had been built between the seventh and eleventh centuries. There was, of course, a hiatus during the Viking settlement period in the second-half of the ninth century, but the acceptance, or imposition, of Christianity in the Viking-controlled North followed not much more than fifty or sixty years later. Many of these pre-Conquest churches have been rebuilt, but in South Yorkshire (and elsewhere) there are a number of church buildings that show architectural or archaeological features which point to an Anglo-Saxon period date. It is worth examining this provision in the county, how we can recognize Saxon churches and where and how surviving fabric manifests itself. As with most things 'Anglo-Saxon', there are many vagaries and uncertainties. What a church was for is perhaps not as straightforward as it might appear; originally these were probably not for the general use of parishioners, as they became later on, but solely the province of the elite for their use and of course for purposes of display amongst the ruling classes.

The structure of the pre-Conquest Church

The structure of the pre-Conquest Church remains fairly obscure until the late-Saxon period, when both Cnut and Aethelred decreed laws of governance. It seems that they were then generally classified as chief minsters, old minsters, manorial (private) churches with burial grounds, field churches without burial grounds and outlying chapels

(Owen, 1979, p.35). However, this was not necessarily the case in the Viking North, and even then the distinctions between these categories of churches remained rather blurred everywhere until after the Norman Conquest (Morris, 1983, p.64). During the ninth to eleventh centuries, there was an acceleration of 'lesser' church building, especially in the south of England, although in the North this was probably on a lesser scale and no doubt did not occur until after the late-tenth century. These manorial churches, as they had become, were patronized and owned by secular lords, taking over many of the pastoral aspects of the old minsters (Blair, 1985, p.104).

Although some churches were known as old minsters, this does not infer any great antiquity for them, but it does imply that they were important central churches and minsters, and they may have existed in Northumbria as early as the later-seventh century but certainly by the eighth and ninth centuries (Morris, 1989, p.131); such may have been the status of the church at Conisbrough. There was a close and obvious relationship between the creation and proliferation of more 'lesser' churches and the fragmentation of the earlier large estates. Apart from the outward display of status and piety through church building, the ownership of ecclesiastical foundations by the lay nobility had financial advantages, whereby the lord of the manor was expected to make a profit from them through, for example, tithes and fees (Loyn, 1984, pp.157–60). Town churches appear in some instances to have been used for commercial purposes as well as for worship, sometimes as taverns or even as marketplaces (Morris, 1989, pp.197–207). Although *Domesday* records churches in the South Yorkshire region which existed by 1086, it is pretty certain that some are missing from the account, especially those churches which were subordinate to a more senior house, as the *Domesday* survey was primarily intent on seeking information strictly for taxation purposes. In most cases, evidence for 'lesser' Saxon-period churches depends only on the chance survival of other documentary evidence (which is very rare, especially in South Yorkshire) or the architectural and archaeological assessment of a building's fabric.

Excavations have suggested that some of the later stone churches were preceded by a graveyard or some small timber structure, and the notion of 'sacred sites' may well have had its part to play in the formation of some church locations (see for example Gilmour and Stocker, 1986). St Helen's Chapel at Barnburgh in South Yorkshire is located next to a spring, also dedicated to St Helen (or locally 'Ellen'), which has a longstanding tradition of healing properties (Cockrell et al., 2011, p.16). A pre-Conquest cross fragment was also found here in the 1990s (Coatsworth, 2008, p.92), suggesting that the site itself had sacred significance, even before the chapel was built. One is reminded that St Augustine was sent to 'Christianize' existing pagan sites in England in the sixth century; a good example of this very practice is the conspicuous prehistoric stone obelisk in the churchyard at Rudston in the East Riding of Yorkshire. It is probable that there are a good many 'pagan' sacred places that became the sites of Christian churches that can no longer be identified as such.

Many church sites were located in or on Roman remains, where these not only served as a convenient 'quarry' for building material (see below) but suggested that those building the churches were the successors of the Roman Empire. The obvious reuse of Roman building components also added an air of antiquity to the otherwise new site. That stone-built churches had timber precursors is a hypothesis which has some following, although it has rarely or never been possible to demonstrate that any set of postholes or artefacts found below those few churches that have been fully excavated were actually ecclesiastical structures. Ryder (1982, p.1) suggests that in South Yorkshire, the first church buildings might have been timber structures and were replaced, sometimes as late as the eleventh century, by stone buildings. Whilst this is possible, we should remember that building in stone was all part of the ideology of the Church of Rome and was adopted wholesale in England from the middle of the seventh century, making the idea of timber church buildings less plausible. Churches built in stone were more about display than they were for worship; to erect a stone church told the world that they (the elite) were part of the wider Holy Roman Empire.

The structure and development of the Anglo-Saxon Church in South Yorkshire is particularly difficult to determine, largely because the earliest reference to any church is in the *Domesday* survey and even that is limited, as described above. By the time that the survey was compiled there had been numerous changes in demography, control and settlement patterns since the first churches were built, and any attempt to provide a sequence of church-building is fraught with problems. The provision of churches mirrored a strictly secular pattern. The mother, or minster, church would be located at the district administrative centre, and as these large old multiple estates became fragmented, the new landholdings eventually would have their own church provision, an evolving process which ended with medieval manorial churches scattered throughout the countryside. Some idea of the sequence of church-building can be implied from what we can reconstruct from the relationships expressed through the *Domesday* survey itself and through the prognosis of earlier centres of administration.

It is contended here that there was practically no settlement south of the River Don until the late-tenth or eleventh century, and thus any church in this area of South Yorkshire is likely to be relatively late in the Saxon period. Therefore, if this argument is accepted, we must look to the north of the river for the earliest church foundations. Of interest is Doncaster; we are fairly certain that there was an administrative centre here by the seventh century, but whether this would have included a church at this early date is uncertain because it seems to have been more a military establishment, well and truly at a frontier and thus in a somewhat unstable location. Much rests on the identity of *Campodonum*, which according to Higham (1993, p.86) referred to the fort and settlement at Doncaster, and according to Bede included a church at the royal residence there (Sherley-Price, 1955, p.132). If *Campodonum* was at Doncaster – and this is a big 'if' – then we can be fairly sure that this would have been

South Yorkshire's first church foundation. The parish church of St George at Doncaster is an imposing building, largely rebuilt in the nineteenth century. It was built over the ruins of *Danum* Roman fort and, to a large extent, respected the orientation of the fort, being at 21 degrees away from a liturgical axis (see Fig. 15). Although many pre-Conquest church buildings were erected upon Roman remains, by no means does this mean that this was exclusive to the post-Roman period, and there is therefore no tangible evidence of a pre-Conquest church here. Having said that, during the tenth century there seems to have been some urbanization and it is highly likely that, at least by the later part of that century, a church stood in Doncaster, but with an unknown status. The *Domesday* account includes Doncaster along with several other settlements under the 'umbrella' of Hexthorpe. A church is mentioned in the entry (Williams and Martin, 1992, p.809), but this may not have been at Hexthorpe as it would seem to imply, possibly referring to the surviving church at Doncaster.

One particular matter which needs to be raised is the possibility of a Roman Christian ecclesiastical provision that survived into the post-Roman period. Ryder (1982, p.12) cites Ecclesfield as a likely candidate for such a building, but this assumption is based largely on the origins of 'eccles' place-names. The origin of 'eccles' has been discussed earlier, where it was concluded that it is unsafe to infer that the use of this 'British West' term for a church necessarily meant a church founded before the arrival of the Anglo-Saxons; it was more a question of local linguistics. However, the evidence from tenth-century stone monuments suggests that there were at least four administrative centres which formed a cohesive unit to the west of the River Dearne (see earlier); arguably, one of these was likely to have been the site of one of South Yorkshire's early churches, and this might well have been Ecclesfield. If this was the case, then we should not necessarily expect it to have been a stone church, built in the familiar Roman style, but more akin to a 'British' foundation, as explained below.

In England, there is proportionally more evidence for pre-Conquest church architecture in eastern counties than in the West. This is no doubt due to the concentration of Anglo-Saxon power in the east of England and the promotion and outward display of piety by the elite. In the more peripheral areas, such as the Pennines, there was perhaps a longer-lasting affinity with British western counties and they were more likely to have embraced Christianity in ways associated with the so-called Celtic Church – timber buildings, small cell structures and so on. Much of South Yorkshire owed its origins as much to the British West as it did to the Anglo-Saxon kingdoms that extracted tribute from this area. The iconography of the stone monuments at Ecclesfield, Penistone, Mexborough and Cawthorne certainly suggests this affinity with the British West, and we should not expect an 'early' church building – as we would expect to recognize it – in this area of South Yorkshire. So Ecclesfield may well have been an early ecclesiastical centre for the region, but it is perhaps no surprise that the architectural evidence is absent.

We can be more confident in the church building at Conisbrough. As far as we can tell, this was an early administrative centre which has produced Anglo-Saxon artefactual evidence from the immediate locale (see earlier). It appears to have held jurisdiction over a wide area, and St Peter's Church has an extensive amount of Anglo-Saxon fabric and architectural components in its present construction, suggesting it once was a superior church. Ryder (1982, p.45) suggests this may be of eighth-century date, based on a typology developed by Taylor and Taylor (1965 and 1978) which is described and critiqued below, but the date of the building is uncertain, although we can be confident that the original building here – and this may not be that in evidence today – would have been one of the earliest, if not *the* earliest, in South Yorkshire.

The sequence of the remainder of church provision in South Yorkshire is difficult to assess. It has often been argued that Anglo-Saxon stone monuments were erected at major ecclesiastical sites, but that is rejected here, as discussed earlier. Although it seems that these were estate centres, they were not necessarily the sites of churches when the monuments were erected. The church at Laughton-en-le-Morthen was probably the first church to be built south of the River Don, but this was not until the end of the tenth century at the very earliest. North of the Don are a number of candidates for churches being built between the eighth and eleventh centuries. Before then, much of southern Yorkshire was perhaps too volatile to expect the general development of church provision to apply to this region. Candidates for relatively early church buildings include those in strategic positions, where the local elite might have expressed their position in this way. Barnburgh and Mexborough could have been such sites along the old frontier, but they may not have been all that 'early'. Having established a small number of minster churches at the administrative centres of the old multiple estates, such as Conisbrough, Ecclesfield and (later) Laughton, church-building is likely to have proliferated after the late-tenth century. These could have included Wath or Bolton-upon-Dearne, Burghwallis, Royston, Penistone, Bradfield and Rotherham, as relatively new estate centres following the fragmentation of the Conisbrough and (perhaps) Ecclesfield multiple estates. South of the River Don, a guess would be the churches at Todwick and Maltby by the eleventh century, formed again from the extensive Conisbrough soke.

In the east of South Yorkshire, the Norman castle at Tickhill suggests that this was a pre-Conquest strategic location, close to the old Roman road from Lincoln to Doncaster (see earlier discussion). As previously mentioned, the Saxon-period estate appears to have been based not on Tickhill, which seems to have developed around the Norman castle site, but on nearby Dadsley. Hey considers that Dadsley All Hallows Church possibly preceded St Mary's Church at Tickhill and is likely to have been a relatively-early church foundation, although again this was almost certainly a centre that developed as part of the former Conisbrough estate, and was therefore later. Interestingly, the foundations of All Hallows Church can be traced near Dadsley Well, 1km or less north of Tickhill (Hey, 1979, p.48).

Elsewhere, pre-Conquest churches in South Yorkshire are likely to have proliferated during the mid- and late-eleventh century, at new manorial holdings such as Thropham, Hooton Pagnall, Hooton Roberts, Thrybergh and Kirk Sandall.

There are several church buildings in South Yorkshire that show some physical evidence for a pre-Conquest date. Some of these are fairly obvious, others not so. In 1982, Peter Ryder conducted a survey of South Yorkshire churches which successfully identified Saxon church fabric at a number of locations, and even though now a little dated, his is a seminal work for this part of England that sadly had been previously neglected. It would be useful to take a little time here to discuss how Anglo-Saxon-period church buildings can be identified. Ryder often refers to 'overlap' church buildings in South Yorkshire, and this is especially a valid observation in this region, where so many church buildings were built in the immediate period on either side of the Norman Conquest that reflected both Anglo-Saxon and burgeoning early-Norman building techniques. Both Anglo-Saxon and Norman stone buildings are referred to as 'Romanesque' in style because the underlying architectural model was that developed during the later-Roman period, which was continued as part of the 'brand' of the succeeding Holy Roman Empire. As a continuing architectural style through the period of the Norman Conquest and thereafter, it is often difficult to identify on which side of the Conquest a church was built. To compound this, recent studies have shown that quarrying was limited in the Anglo-Saxon period and the reuse of Roman building material appears to be much more widespread than previously supposed (see, for example, Eaton, 2000), as discussed below.

The identification of Saxon churches

The identification and especially the dating of Anglo-Saxon churches are fraught with problems. Even on those relatively rare occasions when pre-Conquest architectural evidence does manifest itself, its date is impossible to determine. It seems that building styles, at least in stone during the Anglo-Saxon period, were not determined by any pre-existing blueprint, but by the availability of materials and components with which to build. The nature of church-building also differed from region to region, with Anglo-Saxon churches more easily recognized in some areas than in others. Occasionally, church sites of antiquity (not necessarily Anglo-Saxon) can only be implied by ephemeral indicators such as unusual axes, suggesting alignment with previous Roman buildings. There was, however, another factor that not only determined the scale of church buildings but also continues to confound the dating of pre-Conquest architectural styles: the availability of Roman remains to reuse and the ease of their transportation.

The 1960s saw a landmark publication by Harold and Joan Taylor (1965) which gave an archaeological perspective, as well as an architectural one, to the study of pre-Conquest church buildings. The Taylors developed a dating sequence which saw an evolving style of architectural components, thus enabling some semblance of dating methodology that could be applied to Anglo-Saxon church buildings. To some extent, this was similar to the dating process applied to Anglo-Saxon stone monuments. The Taylors produced a further volume thirteen years later (Taylor and Taylor, 1978) which divided pre-Conquest architecture into three main periods with subdivisions. Perhaps the main criticism levied at the Taylors' work was that many of these dates appeared to be too early, and this was indeed accepted by Harold Taylor in 1978, leaving the discipline less sure of its chronology. More recent studies have compounded this uncertainty as it became increasingly clear that Roman components were reused on a much larger scale than previously realized (see, for example, Stocker, 1990) and that quarrying for fresh stone was rare. One of the most influential studies to follow was that by Eaton (2000), which concluded that the vast majority of Anglo-Saxon church buildings used plundered stone and components from Roman remains.

The reuse of Roman material had two functions. Firstly, the former Roman forts and towns provided a veritable 'builders' yard' for materials, with door and window frames, dressed stone blocks, architectural embellishments and so on all there for the picking, along with the template for building techniques in stone, a medium otherwise unfamiliar to Anglo-Saxon craftspeople. Secondly, the reuse of Roman components had an iconic value; as noted earlier, the Germanics regarded themselves as the successors to the Roman Empire, and the resurrection of Roman-style buildings promoted this claim. But the reuse of Roman material also meant that there was really no true 'Anglo-Saxon' building style in stone, with church buildings of the time simply reflecting the availability and type of Roman material that was used, meaning that Anglo-Saxon architecture cannot be dated by stylistic means. There is indeed a correlation between surviving Anglo-Saxon church buildings and the proximity of former Roman forts and towns. In this respect, communication routes had their part to play, surviving and well-maintained Roman roads and navigable rivers making the transportation of building materials and larger components that much easier (Eaton, 2000). In Yorkshire, Taylor (1961) described a small number of churches with surviving Anglo-Saxon fabric, and not surprisingly they are all located on, or close to, Roman communication routes. Examples include Ledsham (next to Ermine Street), Appleton-le-Street (referring to a settlement on a Roman road) or the church at Skipwith, where all the evidence points to reused Roman material being rafted down the River Ouse, less than 5km to the west of the present church building (Buckland, 2010, p.3).

It would perhaps be useful at this stage to examine the characteristics of pre-Conquest church buildings and why the identification of any surviving Anglo-Saxon fabric can be problematic. Most Anglo-Saxon churches were originally simple, two-cell structures comprising a rectangular nave and a small chancel. Characteristic of Saxon-period buildings is a long, narrow nave, where the ratio between the length and width of this component is greater than that usually found in post-Conquest churches. Pre-Conquest chancels were notably narrower than their Norman successors, and were usually square (roughly) with a relatively narrow arched opening to the nave, but such openings rarely survived subsequent alterations during the Norman and later periods, so as a generality this is uncertain. Occasionally, an addition to the basic structure was a *porticus*, an annexe located on the side of the nave. The function of the *porticus* is less than clear because none have survived above foundation level, although the surviving pre-Conquest part of Laughton church in South Yorkshire may originally have been one of these (Ryder, 1982, p.71). The late Saxon period saw the proliferation of west towers. This appears to have been a monumental statement through which the elite were able to demonstrate both their piety and their wealth by dominating the surrounding countryside. Towers appear to have been synonymous with the development of late-Saxon landholdings that were fragmented from the larger and earlier estates. Because of the scale of this late-Saxon investment in towers, they often survived almost intact (at least at lower levels), even though the nave and chancel were replaced by larger medieval structures.

Later alterations, renovations and rebuilds often destroyed their pre-Conquest predecessor. But in some cases the pre-Conquest fabric – in particular the nave, or part of it – was simply incorporated into the later building by extending the church around the original core. Because of the addition of aisles, larger chancels and the like, surviving pre-Conquest fabric can become hidden, especially if the walls were rendered. In some cases only the nave dimensions are likely indicators of a pre-Conquest foundation, although in some buildings this can be identified from relict architectural components and reused Roman components. Saxon-period door openings had round-arched heads, were unusually tall compared with their width, and many or most were simply doorways plundered from Roman sites. Window openings were small and usually quite high in the walls of the nave compared with those of later medieval buildings, and sometimes survive as small blocked-up arches, as in Conisbrough parish church. This style of window, whilst serving its primary purpose in supplying light into the building, was also intended to preserve the mysteries of the interior. Many of these window arches are referred to as 'Escomb-style' windows, but they again were components plundered from Roman remains (see Fig. 52).

Pre-Conquest wall fabric is probably the most difficult to identify as it can take a variety of forms. Some Saxon-period wall fabric is of ashlar – formed blocks of coursed stone similar to medieval and later construction. Alternatively, the very opposite can be found with 'random rubble' construction, where the stones used are of different shapes and sizes, all roughly fixed in a matrix of thick cement. Between these two extremes are a variety of styles, including semi-coursed and 'herringbone' construction, found also in both Norman and Roman contexts. Random rubble wall fabric is a good indicator of pre-Conquest building, as this sometimes stands in stark contrast with the later medieval fabric. It is assumed that this type of Saxon-period walling was intended to be hidden by external rendering, again a Roman form of decoration, but unfortunately also a technique sometimes

Fig. 52: Roman hypocaust blocks which were reused as the familiar 'Escomb-style' window arches.

used by Norman masons. Eaton's study (2000), which highlighted the wholesale reuse of Roman masonry in the construction of Anglo-Saxon church buildings, describes a process where cartloads of stone were transported, one after another, from a Roman site to the new church under construction. The effects of this can be seen in a phenomenon known as 'banding', under which each cartload was used to build a couple of courses of the wall, followed by the next load and so on. However, each cartload often carried stones of different sizes, which can be seen in bands of varying stone sizes in the elevation of the wall.

Apart from window and door openings, another excellent diagnostic element is the quoins found at the corners of church buildings. A distinctive style appears to have prevailed through most or all of the pre-Conquest period which used megalithic blocks to provide support in these areas. There are two main types of corner quoins, as shown in Fig. 54; both are conspicuous by their comparatively large size. Again, Saxon corner quoins usually reused large Roman blocks, and Roman 'Lewis holes' – a slot cut to lift the stone – can sometimes be detected in them. It is said that there is a regional division between the different styles; those of the 'long-and-short' variety are confined to the old kingdoms of Mercia and Wessex, whereas the side-alternate and the related 'random megalithic' styles are seen as Northumbrian (for example, see Ryder, 1982). In practice, although this does seem to be a general rule, there are the inevitable exceptions; one wonders whether regional variation is simply confused with the type of components available from Roman contexts.

In this review of Anglo-Saxon building styles, it has to be pointed out that the number of surviving Anglo-Saxon churches in England is very small, and even these are incomplete. Most surviving pre-Conquest fabric is found in towers, for example at Barton-on-Humber, Earl's Barton, Barnack and some of the 'town' churches like those in Oxford or York. Surviving Saxon naves and chancels are rare, such as those found at Bradwell-on-Sea, Brixworth, Escomb and Deerhurst. Beyond these few examples, Anglo-Saxon fabric and components largely only manifest themselves through odd surviving

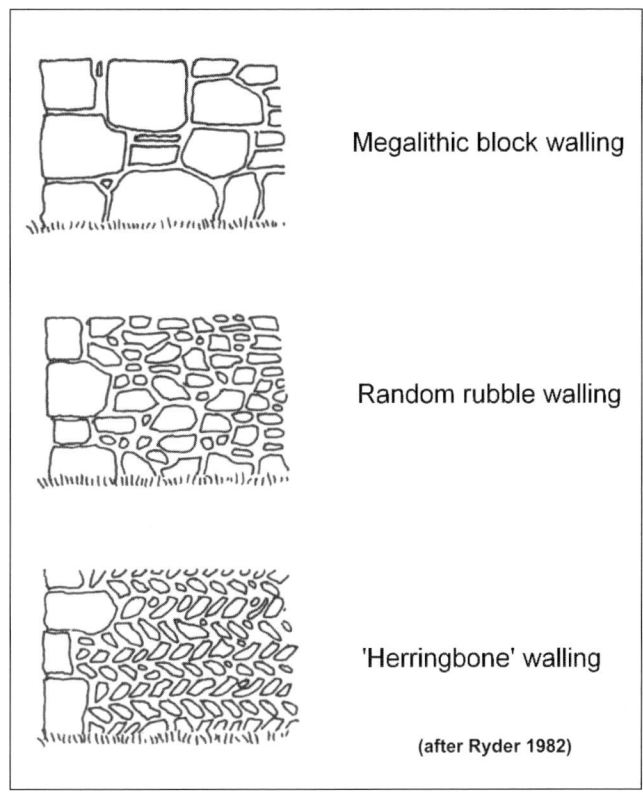

Fig. 53: Wall types (after Ryder, 1982).

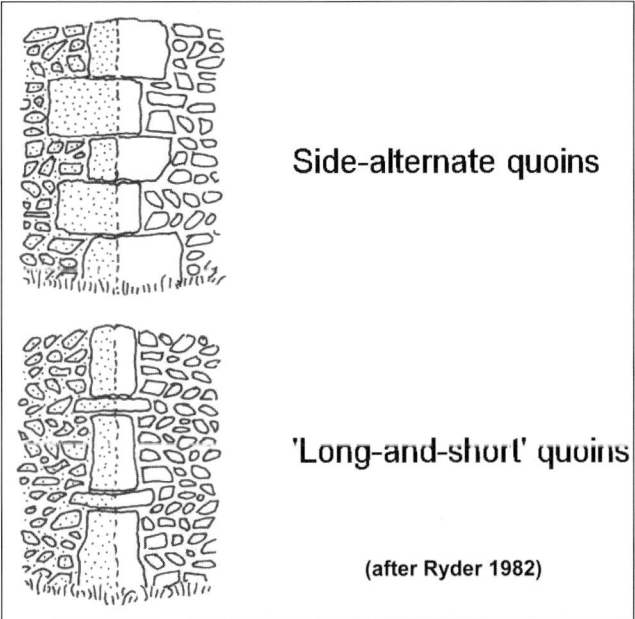

Fig. 54: Corner quoins (after Ryder, 1982).

windows, doors and quoins in subsequently altered buildings. Unlike churches of the later-medieval, decorated or perpendicular styles, Saxon churches do not provide anything like a reasonably-sized database on which to build a reliable typology of stylistic elements, let alone develop a chronological sequence. In short, even if Roman components had not been reused, it is questionable whether there is enough surviving evidence on which to date the buildings.

Review of the Anglo-Saxon churches of South Yorkshire

Table 1: Churches and priests in South Yorkshire mentioned in the Domesday survey.

Location	Description
North of River Don	
Conisbrough	Church and priest
Bolton-upon-Dearne	Church and priest
Brodsworth	Church and priest
Kirk Sandall	Church and priest
Barnby Dun	Church and priest
Littleworth (Rossington)	Church and priest
Tankersley	Church and priest
Cawthorne	Church and priest
Hexthorpe (with Doncaster)	Church and priest
Wildthorpe (near Cadeby and High Melton)	Priest only
South of River Don	
Bramham	Church and priest
Braithwell	Church and priest
Dadsley (with Hellaby and Stainton)	Church and priest
Rotherham	Church and priest
Todwick	Church only
Treeton	Church and priest
Aston	Church and priest
Maltby	Church and priest

Table 1 shows the South Yorkshire churches and priests mentioned in the *Domesday* survey of 1086. As previously mentioned, the *Domesday* survey was only interested in the ability to raise taxes, and not all churches were included. It is difficult to identify why one church was mentioned and another was not. For example, the church at Laughton-en-le-Morthen clearly has an Anglo-Saxon heritage (see below), but it was not mentioned in the *Domesday* account, despite the centre being of prime importance in its region. Meanwhile, presumed lesser churches, such as Todwick, were included, despite the likelihood that they were within the jurisdiction of a more senior church (oddly, in this case, Laughton). So we are left with a scattering of documented pre-Conquest churches and a few other buildings where there is surviving architectural or archaeological evidence for an early building. With regard to the latter, there are limitations to what we might expect that evidence to be, and of course it depends on whether some part of the building has remained untouched for more than 1,000 years and that the evidence is recognizable. There are other factors that have determined the survival and identification of pre-Conquest church fabric in South Yorkshire, very often being its location, as will be explained below.

In South Yorkshire, it is clear that a correlation exists between those locations where Anglo-Saxon fabric survives in church buildings and the proximity of Roman roads, especially Ermine Street and Ryknield Street. These roads seem to have served as routes for transporting building materials from the former Roman forts at Danum and Templeborough. The only exception is Penistone, which is not near a known Roman road (but see the earlier discussion on the Bar Dyke earthwork and the routeway it protected). Here, the evidence is that part of the nave of a pre-Conquest church may survive (Ryder, 1982, p.95). One of the nave corner quoins is part of a reused stone cross shaft, suggesting that the date of the nave is no earlier than the late-tenth century. Fig. 55 shows the distribution of churches containing fabric dating to the Anglo-Saxon period, including those often termed 'overlap' in style, in that the building

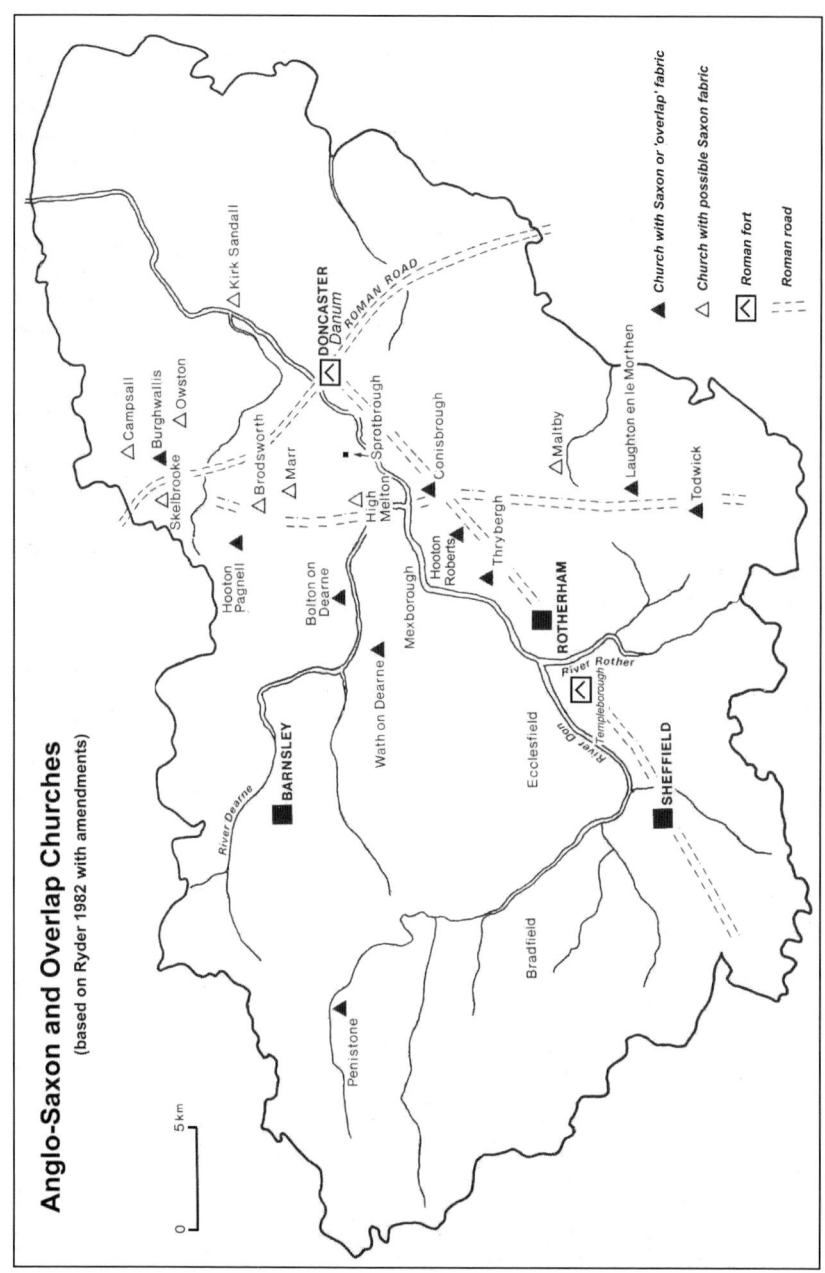

Fig. 55: Surviving Anglo-Saxon and 'overlap' church fabric in South Yorkshire (based on Ryder, 1982).

may have been either late-Saxon or early-Norman (Ryder, 1982). Of course, there would have been more churches in South Yorkshire that had a pre-Conquest foundation but where Anglo-Saxon fabric has not survived. This is especially likely for buildings further away from Roman communication routes, and particularly far from the forts at Templeborough and Danum.

That Anglo-Saxon church builders in South Yorkshire extensively reused Roman masonry and components is beyond question. Buckland points out that several churches in the Doncaster region which are located on, or adjacent to, the Magnesian Limestone ridge include significant quantities of Carboniferous sandstone. At Bolton-upon-Dearne, north of the River Don, on an outcrop of sandstone known as Darfield Rock, the quoins and jambs of the nave use, or rather reuse, a different Carboniferous source, probably recycled from the Roman fort at Templeborough, near Rotherham, which had been abandoned in the early-third century (Buckland, 2010, p.9). The church at Laughton-en-le-Morthen is built predominantly from Magnesian Limestone, but the surviving pre-Conquest fabric now in the north aisle is built from 'Rotherham Red' sandstone, which was undoubtedly plundered from Templeborough fort. St Peter's Church at Conisbrough has a reused Roman sculpture in the south porch (Fig. 56) and some reused decoration in the north wall of the nave, which again most likely is Roman. As noted earlier, a small section of spiralling pattern is built into the church wall at Sprotbrough. Although Coatsworth (2008, p.251) thinks this might be Anglo-Saxon, it is unlike any other design on cross shafts in the region (Sidebottom, 1994) and it is more likely a reused Roman decorative panel or frieze.

The parish church at Burghwallis is equally interesting. Built into the chancel wall is a Roman stone oculus – a small circular opening – that has been reused in the fabric of the building. The plan of the church is unusual; it is slightly trapezoidal, with the tower on a different orientation than the rest of the building (see Fig. 58). According to Ryder (1982, pp.35–39), the nave and much of the

Fig. 56: Roman sculpture at Conisbrough.

Fig. 57: Probable Roman Spiralling pattern reused at St. Mary's, Sprotbrough (from Coatsworth 2008, reproduced by courtesy of the Corpus of Anglo-Saxon Stone Sculpture).

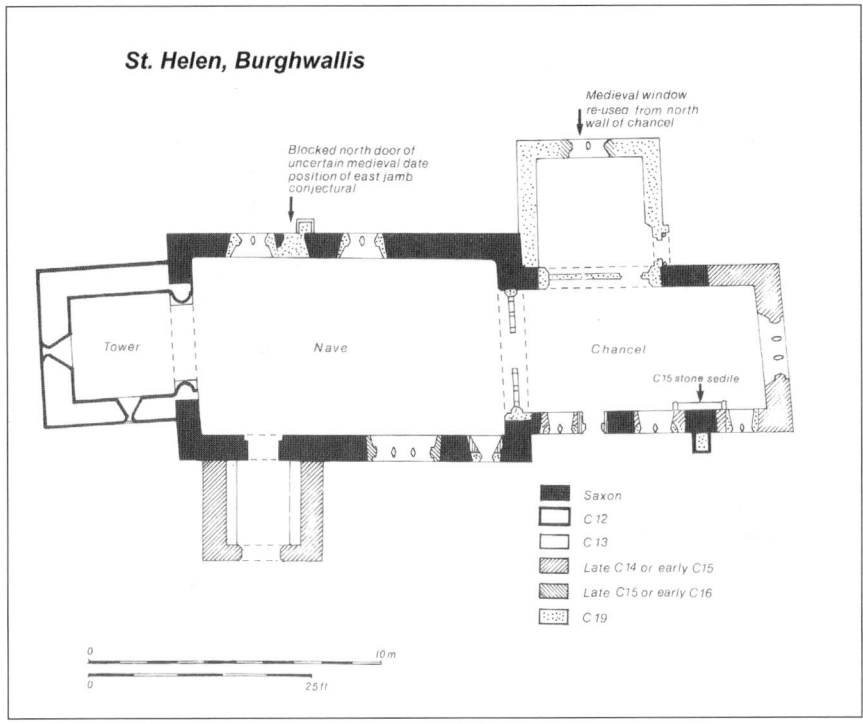

Fig. 58: Burghwallis church plan (after Ryder, 1982).

chancel date from the Anglo-Saxon period, and certainly the quoins, the 'random rubble' and herringbone construction support this view. There is also some banding present in the nave and chancel walls, and odd pieces of terracotta tiling, suggesting this was due to Roman *spoila* being carted in from a convenient source. Burghwallis lies just a few kilometres from Ermine Street, about 8km north of the fort at *Danum* and 3km from a former Roman bathhouse complex at Hampole. Like the chapel at Barnburgh, Burghwallis church is dedicated to St Helen, with a spring rising nearby, and its orientation is 22 degrees away from a true east–west alignment; it could possibly have respected the foundations of a Roman building or some pre-existing structure.

St Peter's at Tankersley shows no fabric that can easily be attributed to the Anglo-Saxon period, although a church is noted in the *Domesday* survey of 1086 (Williams and Martin, 1992, p.810). Again,

Fig. 59: Burghwallis oculus.

the orientation of the church building is well away from a liturgical axis, being as much as 32 degrees from an east–west alignment. In this instance, the church seems to be aligned with a footpath which runs along a series of coaxial field boundaries over some distance,

Fig. 60: Burghwallis wall fabric.

and it is tempting to see this as the vestiges of an ancient routeway which influenced the axis of the building (see Fig. 61). This is not a known Roman road, although an area known as 'Finkle Street' is just 5km away along the same axis.

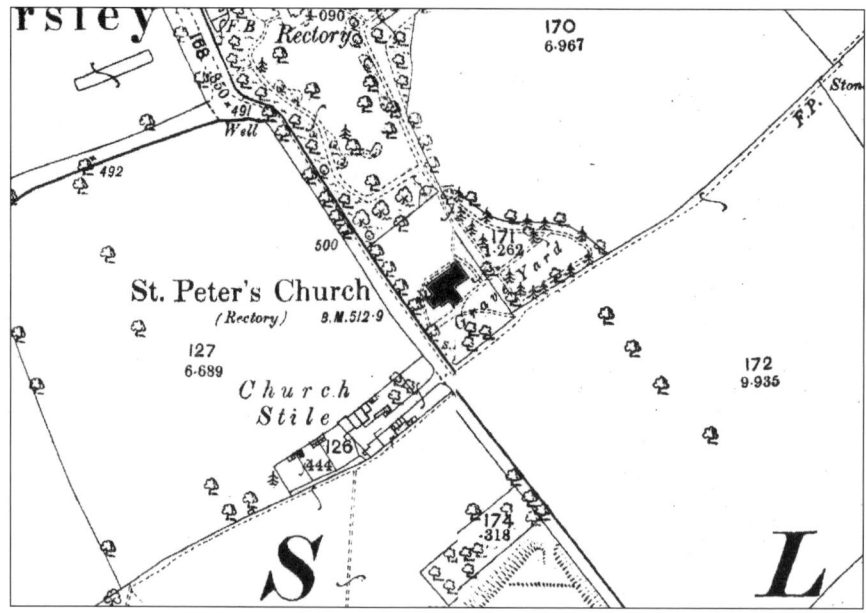

Fig. 61: Tankersley church in 1893 (Ordnance Survey, 1893).

One of the most complete Anglo-Saxon church buildings in South Yorkshire is St Peter's at Conisbrough. Again, this is a building close to the Roman fort at *Danum* and to the road linking it to the fort at Templeborough. The nave and part of the tower date from the Anglo-Saxon period, and according to Ryder (1982, p.52) there is some evidence that the remains of a small, almost square, chancel lies within the later and present chancel fabric. Blocked, 'Escomb'-type windows are visible in the upper part of the nave walls (see Fig. 63), and the size of the nave – large for the period at about 14 metres long – perhaps underlines the pre-Conquest importance of the building.

All Saints' Church at Hooton Pagnall is one of Ryder's 'overlap' churches, although it is most likely a pre-Conquest building using *spoila* from *Danum* Roman fort, given the banding which can be seen in the walls of the nave and tower. Ryder (1982, p.63) sees this as an eleventh-century building and, one would agree, an example of those 'manorial' churches which proliferated between Conisbrough and Doncaster in the late Saxon period. The tower, small nave and part

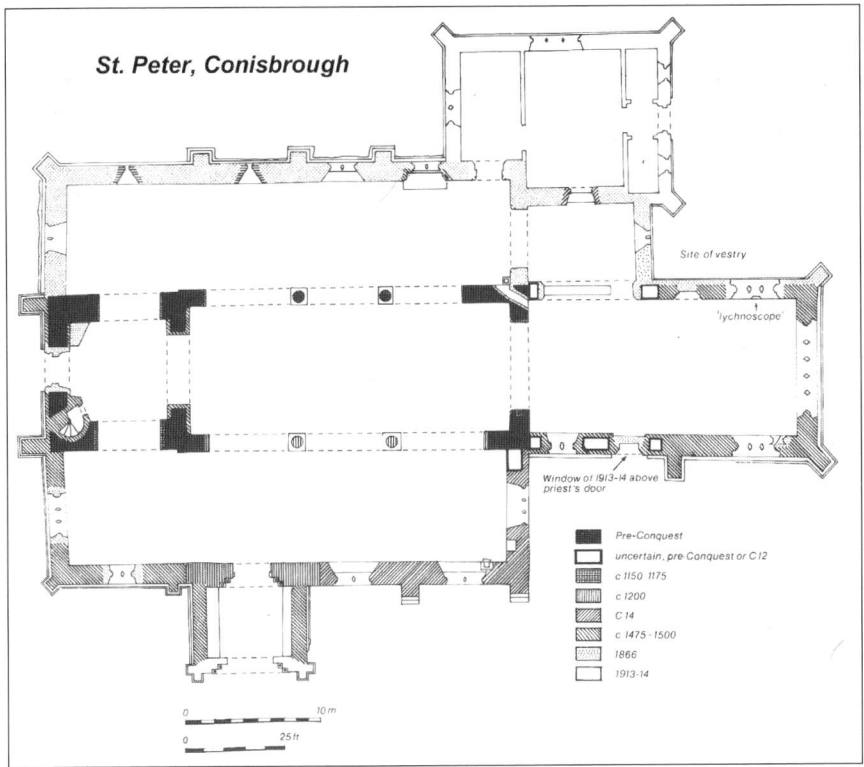

Fig. 62: Plan of St Peter's, Conisbrough (from Ryder, 1982).

of the chancel (again suggesting a roughly square cell) are all pre-Conquest. There is a good example of 'random rubble' masonry used in the walling, with some semi-dressed stones. The nave is small, measuring about 9 metres long, reflecting the church's lesser status compared with Conisbrough, but the tower is disproportionally large, being as wide as the nave and more than 5 metres long, making it typical of late-Saxon towers as described earlier.

All Saints' Church at Laughton-en-le-Morthen has been mentioned above and is largely a twelfth-century Norman building, although Ryder (1982, p.72) suspects at least the core of the tower's footprint is pre-Conquest; the rest of the tower is fourteenth century. However, a western continuation of the north aisle is purely pre-Conquest work, almost certainly using reused Roman components. Ryder thinks this

Fig. 63: Blocked window in the nave wall of Conisbrough church.

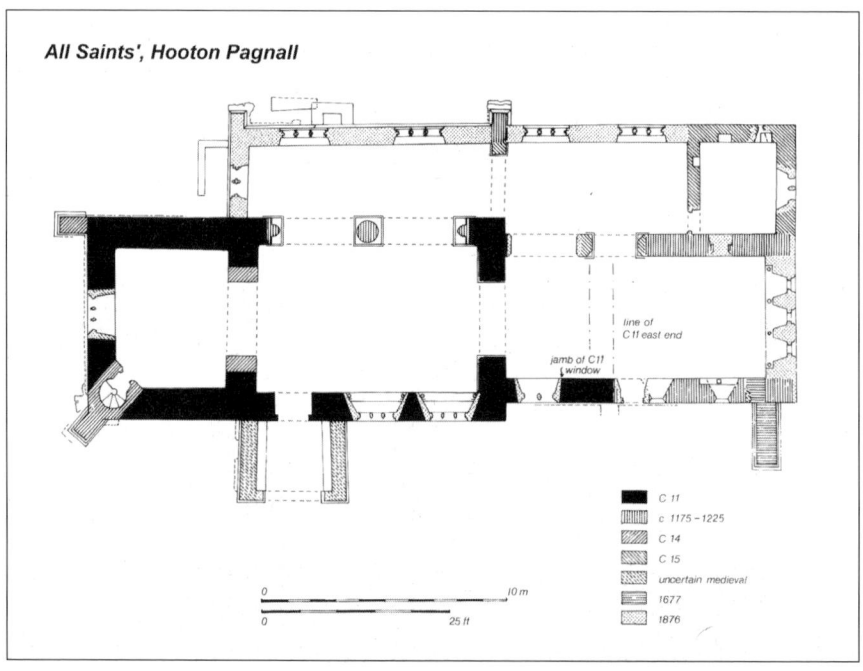

Fig. 64: Plan of All Saints', Hooton Pagnall (after Ryder, 1982).

is a surviving part of a *porticus* with a large external door, which may very well be the case, although given the large side-alternate quoins at its eastern end it could possibly have been the base of an early tower built before the present fourteenth-century structure. The quoins at the western end are no longer visible, and a later and smaller door opening has been built within the larger pre-Conquest doorway. Although the surviving fabric of the nave and chancel suggests a twelfth-century date, the wall fabric is far from uniform. In the main, the wall fabric is rubble using local stone (Magnesian Limestone), consistent with Norman construction. However, there are also quite a number of pieces of 'Rotherham Red' sandstone built into the lower stages of the chancel and in the eastern end of the nave (where it is not obscured by the south aisle). The probability is that the sandstone was reused from an earlier building that most likely was the pre-Conquest structure of which the surviving Anglo-Saxon fabric was once part.

Fig. 65: Surviving Anglo-Saxon doorway at Laughton.

Fig. 66: Possible surviving Anglo-Saxon wall fabric at Laughton.

The Church of St Peter and St Paul at Todwick could be described as another 'overlap' church, with a small, slightly trapezoidal nave about 12 metres in length (Ryder, 1982, p.99), again consistent with one of the relatively-new manorial churches which was most likely part of the fragmentation of the Laughton estate. The nave is constructed from rough-cut stones, with heavy side-alternate corner quoins. There is a blocked Romanesque door opening along the north wall which is probably late Saxon.

St Andrew's Church at Bolton-upon-Dearne boasts a rare survival of 'Mercian-styled' long-and-short corner quoins (see discussion above). The nave is pre-Conquest and is only about 11 metres long, but unusually wide for a pre-Conquest building (some 9 metres). The nave walls are constructed from random rubble and there are several interesting features which probably date from the pre-Conquest period, although there have been many later alterations and insertions. There is a high window in the south wall of the nave, the frame of which is constructed from a single block of stone; it

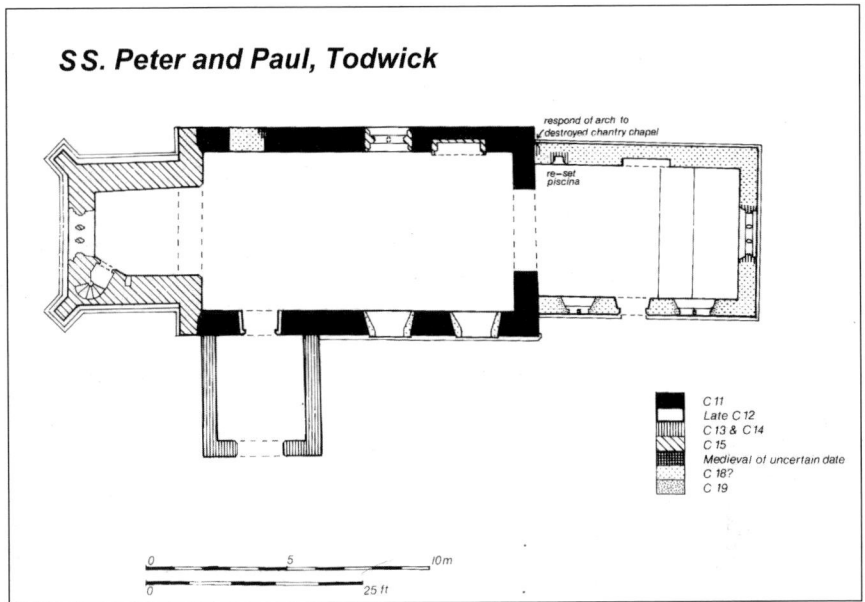

SS. Peter and Paul, Todwick

respond of arch to destroyed chantry chapel

re-set piscina

C 11
Late C 12
C 13 & C 14
C 15
Medieval of uncertain date
C 18?
C 19

0   5   10m
0   25 ft

Fig. 67: Plan of St Peter and St Paul, Todwick (after Ryder, 1982).

is almost certainly a plundered Roman component. A frieze reused in the tower may also be Roman, but could equally be a medieval addition to later additions and alterations. Ryder (1982, p.20) suggests that the Saxon church was built in the eleventh century, and one would agree that it was most likely a relatively-late addition to the provision of churches in what would have been part of the Conisbrough estate.

The Church of St John the Baptist at Hooton Roberts has not been regarded as a Saxon building by previous writers. However, it may be one of those 'overlap' buildings, having a small nave of similar dimensions to those described above; it could have been a late-Saxon manorial church. The nave fabric is interesting and suggests that some of it may have been built from material imported and reused from a Roman context; the church stands on the old Roman road between *Danum* and Templeborough. Ryder offers other examples in South Yorkshire where the evidence for a pre-Conquest church is ephemeral and in many cases inconclusive, such as those at Throapham, Maltby,

Fig. 68: Wall fabric and blocked door, Todwick.

Wath-upon-Dearne or Kirk Sandall (see Ryder, 1982). We should also mention St Wilfred's Church at Hickleton, which in 1984 needed extensive underpinning following mining subsidence. A programme of archaeological excavation was undertaken. This revealed a much

Fig. 69: Bolton quoins.

Fig. 70: Bolton high window.

more complicated sequence than is apparent in the visible church architecture, with the earliest phase dating to around the mid-eleventh century, making this one of the Saxo-Norman 'overlap' churches of South Yorkshire. In the soil deposits beneath the church, a silver penny from AD 905, Saxon and Roman pottery and a Roman brooch pin were found (South Yorkshire HER 00366).

Hickleton church is not mentioned in the *Domesday* survey, although it seems it was in existence by the time the document was compiled in 1086. The surviving structure gives no clue as to its earlier origins; had it not been for the underpinning that was urgently needed and the archaeological investigations that ensued, we would never have known that the site had Anglo-Saxon origins. It provides us with a reminder that there are likely to be other 'Hickletons' in the South Yorkshire landscape – and elsewhere for that matter – and underlines how our knowledge and understanding of the period is developing all the time.

Conclusions

It seems that South Yorkshire throughout the post-Roman, Anglo-Saxon and Viking periods was an area dominated by political events which made its development unique. Topographically, South Yorkshire shared a common economic environment or 'ecozone' with people of a larger region in what became known as the West Riding during the Viking period, one that became typified by hill farming with limited arable production, but well suited to animal rearing. It was a different economic region to that, for instance, of the Vale of York to the east, or the more agriculturally-amenable landscapes of the north Midlands or present-day Lincolnshire. No doubt this difference helped to forge a localized identity which was strictly 'Pennine Yorkshire'. During the Iron Age and Roman periods, South and West Yorkshire were seemingly part of the Brigantian tribal unit or federation which demanded heightened military suppression after the Roman conquest of Britannia. However, it is probable that the southern part of South Yorkshire was part of the *civitas* of the Corieltauvi or Coritani of the north Midlands. This division seems to have been marked largely by the River Don, and after the withdrawal of the Roman military resurrected itself, becoming once again an area of contention.

There is little documentation for these Dark Ages in South Yorkshire, and the archaeological evidence is also limited. It seems that South Yorkshire was used as a buffer zone between the kingdoms of Northumbria and Mercia, with earthworks in the region speaking of an area of potential conflict, both before and after the Roman occupation. The Roman Rig earthworks on the north bank of the River Don may well have been constructed during the pre-Roman Iron Age, but were likely to have been reused during the power struggles that followed Anglo-Saxon reorganization of the political landscape, especially during the sixth and seventh centuries. The earthworks were mirrored by a series of 'burgh' place-names, which adds to the evidence for a fortified line along the same axis. There is evidence that much, or all, of South Yorkshire was in turn under the dominance of the emerging Anglo-Saxon kingdoms of Northumbria and Mercia. Dialectic studies and some artefactual evidence, albeit limited, tells of a strong Mercian presence in South Yorkshire, while the *Elmedsaetna* were included in the document known as the *Tribal Hidage*, which also suggests at least a periodic attachment to Mercia.

The full extent of Germanic settlement in South Yorkshire is unknown, but the evidence suggests that this was minimal and essentially strategic, in that Saxon infiltration was largely focussed on defence of the frontier rather than peaceful settlement. The former Roman fort at Doncaster became pivotal in the control of the region, with the Roman road from Lincoln to Doncaster, and northwards into Northumbria, important in the power struggles between the two kingdoms, several battles being fought along its route. Similar comments can be echoed for the Viking settlement, where any Scandinavian presence appears to have also been strategic, focussed on the Don navigation and important routeways. The area of South Yorkshire south of the River Don was, for several centuries, largely a 'no-go' area, and this is borne out by charter evidence, the distribution of stone monuments in the region and evidence for woodland regeneration; it is perhaps no coincidence that Sheffield has been called Europe's 'greenest' city. Place-name evidence and that from stone monuments indicates that there was a continuing British administration, especially in the west of South Yorkshire, where there is also evidence for Hiberno-Norse settlement. These two groups – one native and the other possibly of indirect Scandinavian descent – seem to have integrated, with co-operation between relatively marginalized groups sharing the same landscape and economy.

The changing political landscape following the Viking settlement of northern England led to a change in the dynamics of the frontier.

This was now further to the south and between two Viking groups with an unknown relationship existing between them, but both facing a common enemy in the West Saxons and their allies. The new frontier became less defendable and almost arbitrary, following minor watercourses, and eventually this line became the county boundary between Yorkshire and Derbyshire. After this, and only then, could South Yorkshire south of the River Don prosper. The new political dynamics between the Viking groups and the eventual conquest by the West Saxons of the Vikings of the North and Midlands enabled the extension of settlement and control to take place in earnest in the southern part of South Yorkshire and neighbouring north-eastern Derbyshire. Freestanding stone monuments of the tenth century provide a tantalizing snapshot of political relationships of the time. We are able to detect both an Anglo-Scandinavian and a native British presence in the control of the county's estates and that the region was composed of small groups, all sharing a commonality through economy and place.

Originally administered from the important centre of Conisbrough, the new areas south of the River Don developed into a small number of late Saxon estates after the tensions of these borderlands had eased. In time these became fragmented, with new landholdings created by the eleventh century. Charter evidence shows that much of this area became subject to external control after the West Saxon conquest of the North, through land acquired by the Saxon Wulfric Spott and evidenced by his will at the beginning of the eleventh century. Together with the introduction of wapentakes and shires and the fragmentation of the old multiple estates, localized control was diluted and reorganized with the formation of later Saxon nucleated settlements, manorial holdings and increased control by the local elite over the peasant farmers. Given this new wealth, local lords invested in church-building, which proliferated in the late Saxon period, leading to a rich architectural and archaeological ecclesiastical heritage in the county. Building in stone was not an Anglo-Saxon or

Scandinavian tradition, and the reuse of Roman material in these early church buildings, for both practical and iconic reasons, is apparent.

The story of South Yorkshire in the Anglo-Saxon and Viking periods – the Dark Ages – is full of conjecture and uncertainty, with the lack of material culture and historic documentation compounding the problem. Nevertheless, what little evidence presents itself is tantalizing, and it is rewarding that the various forms of evidence complement each other to enable a better understanding and sturdier foundations on which to build a synthesis. We are also reminded that our knowledge is evolving all the time, with new discoveries and advances in archaeological techniques that enrich our understanding. Hopefully, this book may go some way to spark interest in an area sadly neglected in terms of research, and will provide some small stimulus to enable others to take this further.

Bibliography

Abrams, L. and Parsons, D.N., 'Place-names and the History of Scandinavian Settlement in England', in J. Hines, A. Lane and M. Redknap (eds), *Land Sea and Home: Proceedings of a Conference on Viking Period Settlement* (Leeds: Maney, 2004), pp.379–431.

Aldred, G., *What are they Worth? An examination of Anglo-Saxon Mercian settlements incorporating the name-element Worth* (unpublished paper, University of Leicester, 2016).

Bailey, R.N., *Viking-Age Sculpture* (London: Collins, 1980).

Barrett, D., 'An Archaeological Resource Assessment of Anglo-Saxon Derbyshire', in *East Midlands Archaeological Research Framework* (Leicester: 2000).

Bassett, S., 'In Search of the Origins of Anglo-Saxon Kingdoms', in S. Bassett (ed.), *The Origins of Anglo-Saxon Kingdoms* (Leicester: Leicester University Press, 1989), pp.3–27.

BGS 2019, The British Geological Survey, http://mapapps.bgs.ac.uk/geologyofbritain/home.html (accessed July 2020).

Biddle, M. and Kjolbye-Biddle, B., 'Repton and the Vikings', in *Antiquity*, vol. 66, issue 250 (1992), pp.36–51.

Black, A. and Black, C., *English Medieval Industries: Craftsmen, Techniques, Products* (eds Blair and Ramsey), (London: Hambleton, 1991), p.13.

Blair, W.J., 'Minster Churches in the Landscape',in D. Hooke (ed.), *Anglo-Saxon Settlements* (Oxford: Blackwell, 1988), pp.35–58.

Boldrini, N., 'When is a border not a border? The Roman Ridge re-evaluated', in C. Cumberpatch, J. McNeil and S. Whiteley (eds), *Archaeology in South Yorkshire 1996–1998* (Sheffield: South Yorkshire Archaeology Service, 1999), pp.101–04.

Breeze, A., 'The Kingdom and Name of Elmet', in *Northern History*, vol. 39:2 (2002), pp.157–71.

Brooks, N., 'The Formation of the Mercian Kingdom', in S. Bassett (ed.), *The Origins of Anglo-Saxon Kingdoms* (Leicester: Leicester University Press, 1989a), pp.159–70.

Buckland, P.C., 'Ragnarök and the stones of York', in J. Sheehan and D. O'Corrain (eds), *The Viking Age: Ireland and the West* (Proceedings of the Fifteenth Viking Congress, 2010).

Buckland, P.C., *Roman South Yorkshire: a source book* (Sheffield: University of Sheffield, 1986).

Buckland, P.C., Buckland, P.I. and Prosser, T., 'Edlington Wood: using Lidar to put ancient fields and old excavations into their contemporary landscape', in *Transactions of the Hunter Archaeological Society*, vol. 29 (2017), pp.84–101.

Buckland, P.C. and Dolby, M.J., 'Fort, Town or Village? The Late Roman Enclosure at Doncaster, South Yorkshire', in *Transactions of the Hunter Archaeological Soc.*, vol. 31 (2021), pp.21–55.

Buckland, P.C., Hey, D., O'Neill, R. and Tyers, I., *The Conisbrough Estate and the southern boundary of Northumbria. Environmental and archaeological evidence from a late sixth/early seventh century structure and a later deer park boundary at Conisbrough, South Yorkshire* (Researchgate.net, 2013; (PDF) Conisbrough with figures. Accessed Dec. 2020).

Buckland, P.C. and Magilton, J.R., *The archaeology of Doncaster* (Oxford: British Archaeological Reports, British Series, 1986), p.148.

Buckland, P.C., Magilton, J.R. and Dolby, M.J., 'The Roman Pottery Industries of South Yorkshire: A Review', in *Brittania*, vol. 11 (1980), pp.145–64.

Burch, P.J.W., *The Origins of Anglo-Saxon Kingship* (unpublished PhD Thesis, University of Manchester, 2015).

Cameron, K. (ed.), *Place-name Evidence for Anglo-Saxon Invasion and Scandinavian Settlement* (English Place-name Soc., 1975a).

Cameron, K., 'Eccles in English Place-names', in K. Cameron (ed), *Place-name Evidence for Anglo-Saxon Invasion and Scandinavian Settlement* (1975b), pp.1–7.

Campbell, J., *The Anglo-Saxons* (London: Penguin, 1991).

Chadwick, A.M., *The Iron Age and Romano-British Periods. Draft section produced for the South Yorkshire Archaeological Research Framework* (Historic England and the South Yorkshire Archaeology Service, 2019).

Clarke, D., *The Head Cult: tradition and folklore surrounding the symbol of the severed human head in the British Isles* (unpublished PhD thesis, University of Sheffield, 1998).

Coatsworth, E., *Corpus of Anglo-Saxon Stone Sculpture. Vol. VIII: Western Yorkshire* (Oxford: Oxford University Press/British Academy, 2008).

Cockrell, T., Cumberpatch, C., Rylatt, J., Merrony, C. and Fenwick, H., *Fieldwork at St Helen's chapel, Barnburgh, South Yorkshire August 2011* (Brodsworth Archaeology Group, 2011).

Collingwood, W.G., *Angles, Danes and Norse in the district of Huddersfield* (Huddersfield: Tolson Museum, 1921).

Collingwood, W.G., *Northumbrian Crosses of the Pre-Norman Age* (London: Faber and Gwyer, 1927).

Cumberpatch, C., *Anglo-Saxon and early medieval pottery manufacture and use in Doncaster and surrounding areas: a preliminary review* (unpublished paper for the Doncaster Pottery Conference, 2016).

Cumberpatch, C., *Recent Work on Medieval Pottery in South Yorkshire* (unpublished paper for Dearne Valley Archaeology Society, 2011).

Dark, K., 'Epigraphic, Art-historical and Historical Approaches to the Chronology of Class I Inscribed Stones', in N. Edwards and A. Lane (eds), *The Early Church in Wales and the West* (Oxford: Oxbow, 1992), pp.51–61.

Davies, W. and Vierck, H., 'The Contexts of Tribal Hidage: Social Aggregates and Settlement Patterns', in *Frumittelalterliche Studien 8* (Berlin: De Gruyter, 1974), pp.223–93.

Dearne, M.J., *The Economy of the Roman South Pennines with particular reference to the lead extraction industry in its national context* (unpublished PhD thesis, University of Sheffield, 1990).

Downham, C., '"Hiberno-Norwegians" and "Anglo-Danes": anachronistic ethnicities and Viking-Age England', in *Mediaeval Scandinavia* 19 (2009), pp.139–69.

Eaton, T., *Plundering the Past: Roman Stonework in Medieval Britain* (Stroud: Tempus, 2000).

Everson, P. and Stocker, D., *Corpus of Anglo-Saxon Stone Sculpture. Vol. XII: Nottinghamshire* (Oxford: Oxford University Press/British Academy, 2016).

Faull, M., 'British Survival in Anglo-Saxon Northumbria', in Lloyd Laing (ed.), *Studies in Celtic survival* (British Archaeological Report 37, 1977).

Faull, M and Moorhouse, A (eds), *West Yorkshire: an Archaeological Survey to AD. 1500: Vol. 1* (Wakefield: West Yorkshire Metropolitan County Council, 1981).

Featherstone, P., 'The Tribal Hidage and the Ealdormen of Mercia', in M.P. Brown and C.A. Farr (eds), *Mercia: an Anglo-Saxon Kingdom in Europe* (2001), pp.23–34.

Garmonsway, G.N., *The Anglo-Saxon Chronicle* (trans. Garmonsway) (London: Dent,l 1953).

Gelling, M., *The West Midlands in the Early Middle Ages* (Leicester: Leicester Univ. Press, 1992).

Gilmour, B.J. and Stocker, D., 'St Mark's Church and Cemetery', *Archaeology in Lincoln* XVIII (London: CBA, 1986).

Griffiths, D., 'The north-west Frontier', in N.J. Higham and D.H. Hill (eds), *Edward the Elder* (London: Routledge, 2001), pp.167–87.

Grigg, E., *Warfare, Raiding and Defence in Early Medieval Britain* (Ramsbury: Robert Hale, 2018).

Guilbert, G. and Taylor, C., *Grey Ditch, Bradwell, Derbyshire* (unpublished Preliminary Excavation Report on behalf of Trent and Peak Archaeological Trust, 1992).

Hadley, D., 'Burial practices in northern England', in S. Lucy and A. Reynolds (eds), *Burial in Early Medieval England and Wales* (Routledge: Soc. Med. Arch. Monograph 17, 2002), pp.209–28.

Hadley, D.M., 'Multiple Estates and the Origin of the Manorial Structure of the Northern Danelaw', in *Journal of Historical Geography*, 22, 1 (1996), pp.3–15.

Hart, C.R., *The Early Charters of Northern England and the North Midlands* (Leicester U-P, 1975).

Hart, C.R., 'The Kingdom of Mercia', in A. Dornier (ed.), *Mercian Studies* (Leicester U-P, 1977), pp.43–61.

Hart, C., *The North Derbyshire Archaeological Survey to AD 1500* (Derbyshire Archaeological Society, 1981).

Hart, C.R., 'The Tribal Hidage', in *Transactions of the Royal Historical Society*, Fifth Series, vol. 21 (1971), pp.133–57.

Hawkes, J. and Sidebottom, P., *Corpus of Anglo-Saxon Stone Sculpture. Vol. XIII: Derbyshire and Staffordshire* (Oxford: Oxford University Press/British Academy, 2018).

Henson, D., *Place-names and the Anglian Takeover of Elmet* (unpublished paper, Academia, 2020, Academia.edu).

Hey, D., *A History of Yorkshire: County of the Broad Acres* (Lancaster: Carnegie Publishing, 2011).

Hey, D., *Historic Hallamshire* (Ashbourne: Landmark, 2002).

Hey, D., *Medieval South Yorkshire* (Ashbourne: Landmark Publishing, 2003).

Hey, D., *The Making of South Yorkshire* (Ashbourne: Moorland, 1979).

Hey, D., 'Yorkshire's Southern Boundary', in *Northern History 37*: 1 (2000), pp.31–47.

Higham, N.J., 'Northumbria's Southern Frontier: a review', in *Early Medieval Europe* 14 (4) (2006).

Higham, N.J., *The Convert Kings: Power and Religious Affiliation in Early Anglo-Saxon England* (Manchester: Manchester University Press, 1997).

Higham, N.J., *The Kingdom of Northumbria AD 350–1100* (Stroud: Sutton, 1993a).

Higham, N.J., *The Origins of Cheshire* (Manchester: Manchester University Press, 1993b).

Higham, N.J. and Ryan, M.J., *The Anglo-Saxon World* (Yale University Press, 2013).

Historic England, *The National Heritage List* (Listed Entries and Scheduled Monuments in England, 2020).

Hodges, R., *The Anglo-Saxon Achievement* (London: Duckworth, 1989).

Hodges, R., 'Notes on the Medieval Archaeology of the White Peak', in R. Hodges and K. Smith (eds), *Recent Developments in the Archaeology of the Peak District.* Sheffield Archaeological Monographs 2 (Sheffield Academic Press, 1991), pp.111–22.

Institute For Name-Studies, (University of Nottingham, 2019), http://kepn.nottingham.ac.uk/map/county/Derbyshire (accessed July 2019).

Jefferys, T., *1771 Map of Yorkshire by Thomas Jefferys* (Sheffield Archives), https://www.picturesheffield.com/maps.php?file=011 (accessed September 2020).

Jones, G.R.J., 'Early Territorial Organisation in Gwynedd and Elmet', in *Northern History*, vol. X (1975), pp.3–27.

Kirby, D.P., *The Earliest English Kings* (London: Unwin Hyman, 1991)

Kirby, D.P., 'Welsh Bards and the Border', in A. Dornier (ed.), *Mercian Studies* (Leicester: Leicester Univ. Press, 1977), pp.31–42.

Kolb, E., 'Elmet: a Dialect Region in Northern England', in *Anglia – Zeitschrift für englische Philologie,* vol 91 (1973), pp.285–313.

Lang, J.T., *Corpus of Anglo-Saxon Stone Sculpture, Vol. III – York and Eastern Yorkshire* (Oxford: British Academy, 1991).

Loveluck, C., 'The Archaeology of Post-Roman Yorkshire, AD 400 to 700: overview and future directions for research', in

T. Manby, S. Moorhouse and T. Ottaway (eds), *The Archaeology of Yorkshire: an assessment at the beginning of the 21st century* (Yorkshire Archaeological Society, Occasional Paper No. 3, 2003), pp.151–70.

Loyn, H.R., *The Governance of Anglo-Saxon England, 500–1087* (London: Arnold, 1984).

Margary, I.D., *Roman Roads in Britain* (third edition) (London: John Baker, 1973).

Mason, A. and Williamson, T., 'Ritual Landscapes in Pagan and early Christian England', in *Fragments*, vol. 6 (2017).

McCarthy, M. and Paterson, C., 'Viking-Age Site at Workington, Cumbria: interim statement', in S.E. Harding, D. Griffiths and E. Royles (eds), *In Search of Vikings: interdisciplinary approaches to the Scandinavian Heritage of the North-West* (London: CRC Press, 2014), pp.127–36.

McKinley, J.I., 'A Conversion-Period Cemetery at Woodlands, Adwick-le-Street, South Yorkshire', in *Yorkshire Archaeological Journal*, 88:1 (2016), pp.77–120.

Morris, R.K., *Churches in the Landscape* (London: Dent, 1989).

Morris, R.K., *The Church in British Archaeology* (Oxford: CBA, 1983; Res. Rep. 47).

Nash-Williams, V.E., *The Early Christian Monuments of Wales* (Cardiff: Univ. of Wales Press, 1950).

Ordnance Survey, *Roman Britain: south sheet* (Southampton: Ordnance Survey, 2011).

O'Sullivan, D., 'Changing Views of the Viking Age', in *Medieval History*, vol. 2, No. 1 (Bangor: Headstart, 1992), pp.3–13.

Ottaway, P., *Research Framework for South Yorkshire's Historic Environment: Roman* (unpublished document, South Yorkshire Archaeology Service, 2019).

Owen, D., 'Chapelries and Rural Settlement: an examination of some of the Kesteven Evidence', in P. Sawyer (ed.), *English Medieval Settlement* (London: Arnold, 1979), pp.35–40.

Parker, M., 'Ecclesall, a Clue to the Topography of Early Hallamshire', in *Transactions of the Hunter Archaeological. Soc.*, vol. 13 (1985), pp.10–22.

Parker, M.S., 'Some Notes on the Pre-Norman History of Doncaster', in *Yorkshire Archaeological Journal*, vol. 59 (1987), pp.29–43.

Redmonds, G., *Slaithwaite Places and Place-names* (Huddersfield: G.R. Books, 1988).

Roberts, I., 'Rethinking the Archaeology of Elmet', in F.K. Haarer (ed.), *AD 410: The History and Archaeology of Late and Post-Roman Britain* (Soc. For the Promotion of Roman Studies, 2018), pp.182–94.

Roffe, D., *The Derbyshire Domesday* (Matlock: Derbys. Museum Service, 1986).

Ross, C., Gardiner, L.F., Brogan, G. and Russ, H., 'Post-Roman crop production and processing: Archaeological evidence from Goldthorpe, South Yorkshire', in *Environmental Archaeology*, 22:3 (2017), pp.233–46.

Rotherham, I. and Harrison, K., 'History and ecology in the reconstruction of the South Yorkshire fens: past, present and future', in *Proceedings of the IALE Conference, Water and the Landscape: The Landscape Ecology of Freshwater Ecosystems* (2006), pp.8–16.

Ryder, P.F., *Saxon Churches in South Yorkshire* (Sheffield: South Yorkshire County Archaeology Service, 1982).

Sawyer, P.H., 'The Charters of Burton Abbey and the Unification of England', in *Northern History* 10 (1975), pp.28–39.

Sawyer, P., *Anglo-Saxon Lincolnshire* (Lincoln: The History of Lincolnshire Committee, 1998).

Sherley-Price, L., *Ecclesiastical History of the English People*, Bede (trans.) (London: Penguin, 1955).

Sidebottom, P.C., *An Archaeological Desktop Assessment of land off Everton Sluice Lane, Everton, Nottinghamshire* (unpublished report, Phil Sidebottom Archaeological Consultancy, 2015).

Sidebottom, P.C., *An Archaeological Desktop Assessment of Woodland at Lady Cannings Plantation, Ringinglow, Sheffield* (unpublished report, 2002).

Sidebottom, P.C., *Pecsaetna: people of the Anglo-Saxon Peak District* (Oxford: Oxbow Books/Windgather Press, 2020).

Sidebottom, P.C., *Schools of Anglo-Saxon Stone Sculpture in the North Midlands* (unpublished PhD. Thesis, Sheffield University, 1994).

Sidebottom, P.C., 'Stone Crosses of the Peak and the "Sons of Eadwulf"', in *Derbyshire Archaeological Journal* 119 (1999), pp.206–19.

Sidebottom, P.C., 'The Derwent Cross-shaft: Discovery and Excavation 1991', in *Transactions of the Hunter Archaeological Society*, vol. 17 (1993), pp.9–18.

Sidebottom, P.C., *The Early Church in Derbyshire: a study of the development of Anglo-Saxon Church Building* (unpublished study report for the Derbyshire Archaeological Advisory Committee, 2008).

Sidebottom, P.C., 'The Ecclesfield cross and "Celtic" survival', in *Transactions of the Hunter Archaeological Society*, 19 (1997), pp.43–55.

Sidebottom, P.C., 'Viking Age Stone Monuments and Social Identity', in J.D. Richards and D.M. Hadley (eds), *Cultures in Contact* (Turnhout, Belgium: Brepols, 2000).

Smith, A.H., *The Place-names of the West Riding of Yorkshire; part 1, Lower and Upper Strafforth and Staincross Wapentakes* (English Place-name Society, vol. XXX, Cambridge University Press, 1961).

Smyth, A.P., *Scandinavian York and Dublin: the History and Archaeology of Two Related Viking Kingdoms* (Dublin: Irish Academic Press, 1979).

Speed, G. and Walton-Rogers, P., 'A Burial of a Viking Woman at Adwick-le-Street, South Yorkshire', in *Medieval Archaeology* vol. 48, issue 1 (2004), pp.51–90.

Stattel, J., *Re-evaluating the Scale of Viking Settlement in England: the Impact of Recent Archaeology on the Danelaw Debate* (unpublished MPhil essay, University of Cambridge, 2020).

Stein, S., *Research Framework for South Yorkshire's Historic Environment: the Early Medieval Period* (unpublished document, South Yorkshire Archaeology Service, 2019).

Stocker, D. (with P. Everson), 'Rubbish Recycled: a study of the Re-use of Stone in Lincolnshire', in D. Parsons (ed.), *Stone Quarrying and Building in England: AD 43–1525* (Chichester: Phillimore, 1990), pp.83–101.

Taylor, C.M., 'Elmet: Boundaries and Celtic Survival in the Post-Roman Period', in *Medieval History* vol. 2, no. 1 (Bangor: Headstart, 1992), pp.111–29.

Taylor, H.M., 'Anglo-Saxon Churches in Yorkshire', in A. Small (ed.), *The Fourth Viking Congress* (1961), pp.56–66.

Taylor, H.M. and Taylor, J., *Anglo-Saxon Architecture*, vols 1 & 2 (Cambridge: Cambridge University Press, 1965).

Taylor, H.M. and Taylor, J., *Anglo-Saxon Architecture*, vol. 3 (Cambridge: Cambridge University Press, 1978).

Taylor, J., 'The Roman Period', in N.J. Cooper (ed.), *The Archaeology of the East Midlands* (University of Leicester, 2006).

Thomas, C., *Britain and Ireland in Early Christian Times* (London: Thames and Hudson, 1971).

Unwin, T., 'Towards a Model of Anglo-Scandinavian Settlement in England', in D. Hook (ed.), *Anglo-Saxon Settlements* (Oxford: Blackwell, 1988), pp.77–98.

Van De Noort, R., 'Exploring Our Past in the Humber Wetlands', in T. Manby, S. Moorhouse and T. Ottaway (eds), *The Archaeology of Yorkshire: an assessment at the beginning of the 21st century* (Yorkshire Archaeological Society, Occasional Paper No. 3, 2003), pp.255–60.

Waddington, C., 'A forgotten frontier? Investigations at Whirlow Hall Farm, Sheffield', in *Transactions of the Hunter Archaeological Society*, vol. 29 (2017), pp.8–57.

Welch, T.C., 'Road Remains at Burbage and Houndkirk Moors, Sheffield – a possible Roman road', in *Yorkshire Archaeological Journal*, vol. 56 (1984), pp.27–31.

Williams, A. and Martin, G.H., *Domesday Book* (London: Penguin, 1992).

Williams, H., 'Remembering Elites. Early Medieval Stone Crosses as Commemorative Technologies', in *Arkæologi i Slesvig Archäologie in Schleswig*, Sonderband Det 61. Internationale Sachsensymposion 2010 (Haderslev, Denmark), pp.13–31.

Wood, P.N., 'On the Little British Kingdom of Craven', in *Northern History*, vol. 32, issue 1 (1996), pp.1–20.

Woolf, A., 'Caedualla *Rex Brettonum* and the Passing of the Old North', in *Northern History* XLI:1 (2004).

Index

191